DARE TO
SEE

DARE TO SEE

Discovering God in the Everyday

KATIE BROWN

TV Host and Bestselling Author

New York   Nashville

FaithWords
Hachette Book Group
1290 Avenue of the Americas, New York, NY 10104
faithwords.com
twitter.com/faithwords

First Edition: September 2019

FaithWords is a division of Hachette Book Group, Inc. The FaithWords
name and logo are trademarks of Hachette Book Group, Inc.

The publisher is not responsible for websites (or their content) that are not
owned by the publisher.

The Hachette Speakers Bureau provides a wide range of authors for speaking events.
To find out more, go to www.HachetteSpeakersBureau.com or call (866) 376-6591.

Library of Congress Cataloging-in-Publication Data has been applied for.

ISBNs: 978-1-5460-3575-6 (hardcover), 978-1-5460-1730-1 (hardcover, special signed
edition), 978-1-5460-1731-8 (hardcover, special signed edition),
978-1-5460-3574-9 (ebook)

Printed in the United States of America

LSC-C

10 9 8 7 6 5 4 3 2 1

To Meredith Hyatt Corbin,
who was born from my heart after much prayer
You, my love, are truly heaven sent

Contents

Introduction

I have been blessed.

When I feel lonely, I look to God.

When I feel happy, I look to God.

When I am ashamed, I look to God.

When I feel overwhelmed, I look to God.

When I am bursting with joy, I look to God.

When I am all choked up because I feel so warm and fuzzy and full of light, I look to God.

I have been blessed with an intimate walk with God from a young age.

We are partners and collaborators, He and I.

He leads. I walk.

He says jump. I leap.

I turn away.

He jumps in my path and pulls me forward.

I was and still am amazed by the unconditional love and acceptance and celebration I feel shining on me from on high.

No matter what my condition:

Middle child

Struggling teen

Newcomer

Champion

Lover

Mother

TV personality

Loser

Loner

Sister

Wife

I get my walking papers, and find my way by following His beam.

He meets me where I am over and over again.

How?

How, you ask?

How do I know?

Because God is BIGGER than I am.

Deeper than I am.

Better than I am.

He is constant and relentless.

And He always knows best.

My God whispers, He yells, He shines, He cajoles, He pleads, He giggles.

I find Him in the most unexpected places, the most hysterical of situations, in many somber moments.

In *Dare to See*, I want to share with you some of the points in my life where I have been blessed with God's grace,

in obvious ways,

in subtle ways,

and always in definitive ways.

These moments have shaped my character, my heart, my life's

path, and my soul's journey. They have touched my being in ways unimaginable.

Sometimes His road map has been in plain sight.

Other times I have run from it.

Sometimes it has been a joy to receive.

Other times it has been revealed through heartbreaking moments.

Whether I am hiding from it or seeking it, it always finds me in a place I have come to know as the space between.

It is my hope that through sharing these tales, I can help you learn how to develop that muscle of recognition. You can improve your talent of dancing closer with faith, by opening up and into His care and love and direction and conversations with you in the simplest, everyday details.

I have been blessed.

I am a cook, a crafter, a life stylist, a professional homemaker. I have spent twenty years teaching domestic how-to that attempts to improve people's everyday home life.

Today I hope that through the art of storytelling I can reveal another layer of how to improve your everyday life by walking closer as you experience God's grace in your own space between.

I hope that you may be able to hear my voice as you read.

I hope that you might feel my heart as you read.

I hope that you might know my desperate need for you to understand God better as you read.

It is my prayer that these stories will move you to understand you are never alone.

It is my prayer that these stories will inspire you to be on the lookout for your blessings.

It is my prayer that you will gain insight into how to recognize His message created just for you and with you.

God has a how-to plan for you that is bigger, better, and more fulfilling than you or I could ever imagine.

His step-by-step instructions are right there, waiting for you.

You just have to seek, and you shall find.

DOUBT

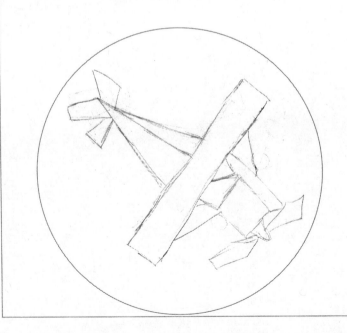

a bathtub

And your ears shall hear a word behind you, saying, "This is the way, walk in it," when you turn to the right or when you turn to the left.

ISAIAH 30:21 ESV

I had given myself a tight deadline to come up with the title and subtitle for this book. For some reason, I really believed a title would shape the direction, the substance, the way I would hug the narrative as I wrote. I felt, if I could nail the title, I would know how to proceed or even to proceed with the lofty goal of trying to highlight my life's powerful moments with God by writing simple essays and turning them into a book. I prayed. I cried. I thought I had it. I did not. I would write words on a big white board, hoping to find a combo that would stick.

I would stop mid conversation, turn to my husband, and blurt out a title. I went to bed thinking about it. I woke up daydreaming about it. How could these collections of mismatched stories have a through-line, a theme, that would be universal enough to fit under one title, or for that matter, universal enough to mean anything to anyone else . . . other than to me.

I was certain the key was in that title, yet what was it? I looked to other authors, authors I had never heard of, but some whom my God-loving mom knew all about. Along the way, I stumbled upon and introduced myself to many fantastic messengers. I read, hoping just one of them might give me a clue:

Lauren Winner's *Girl Meets God*
Rob Bell's *The Holy Shift Tour*
WOW! Those are good titles.
How about, *God Talks to Girl*? No, too close.
All right, *God Is Everywhere Even in the Drive-Through*? Nope, a
  bit too cheeky.

It was Sunday night. I was feeling defeated. Frankly, I was feeling even a bit silly. Who was I to think I could write a book about faith? So, I did what I do on many a Sunday night. I drew a bath for my younger daughter, Meredith, and myself. We crawled in and began talking, laughing, soaking. At one point, as we cuddled together, feeling soothed by the wet warm water, out of the blue Meredith sang in my ear: "And you can find me in the space between." I shouted out to my husband, William. This was a dangerous move because he had just settled in to watch *60 Minutes*. Interrupting him could unnerve him, to say the least. But he dutifully came to the edge of the bathtub . . .

"*The Space Between*?" I sheepishly asked.

Meredith said, "That is what I just said."

"*I know*," I said.

William said, "I LIKE IT!"

The Space Between.

Later, I asked Meredith why she was singing that line. She said it was from a Disney movie, *Descendants 2* (not to be confused with *Descendants 1*, which evidently, according to Meredith, is not as good). Meredith explained that the two main characters were supposed to get married, but instead became separated on different planets. The characters were searching for each other. During the search they came upon something like a fake magic wand and a dog eating a pill that made him tell the truth about a vest that made him look fat. Then, the song "Space Between" began to play.

Of course it did!

At this point and time, I felt just as turned around and lost as the two main characters; I, too, was lost on a new planet that may as well have been full of the vest-wearing dogs and wand-wielding witches.

I am a toast-making, curtain-hanging, vapid TV personality who for some reason felt I was being guided to write a book about the biggest, bestest thing life had given me...faith, a faith that was illuminated by a series of God moments.

Yet as the weekend was coming to an end, my self-doubt was looming large. I thought I was nowhere, until it turned out I was somewhere. I was in *the space between* and Meredith's soft simple song was with me in that space between. A space where God lives with me and...with you. A space where if you look closely enough and really listen, God will take your hand and somehow guide you to the light.

Faith
God
Peace
Answers

The word is right there in plain view where you least expect it. The space between can be anywhere and everywhere. It is:

solemn
freeing
caring
magical
mystical
heavenly,

and can never be found by using your GPS.

It is a feeling, a sense, a calm, a light, a love that will touch you in a place and at times when you need it most. And it is lying right there in the last place you would expect to see or hear it.

The space between is:

small
and powerful
and meaningful
and everything.

So, lean into this space. Bend down low, get up close, focus and listen to the nooks and crannies of God's world to see what you are meant to see, to feel what you are meant to feel.

God's son was born in a manger, the humblest of places. The space between is not a castle or a gilded chariot. It is a soft, subtle place where everyone can travel if they just turn their head and heart ever so slightly. The good, the bad, and the ugly can be made more meaningful if we just shift subtly and tune into God's how-to instructions that are put right in front of us every day and in every way.

No, I did not, in the end, use *The Space Between* as my title.

Why?

Because as I began to write, I realized that living in the space between takes courage and commitment. I realized that the space between was a daring place to live. Seeing what God has laid out for you to grab on to takes might. Hence, *Dare to See* seemed to have the strength I hoped my stories would generate.

However, it was the title that I used to get the book sold to my publisher. It was the title I used when people asked me what I was writing. It was the title that I had in my mind as I gathered the stories I would highlight.

Most important, this title was my ticket to travel to the private space where I experienced and held all my moments that illuminated my walk with God.

A private space that was made more real by the words: The Space Between. A private space that allows me to stand nearer to the love of the Holy, that gives me the calm and energy and understanding I need to find my joy.

Begin looking for your space between, and dare to see what God wants to show you.

For Further Reflection

How has doubt impacted you as you endeavored to achieve
  something meaningful?
How does God help your boldness in this experience?
How is that endeavor a gift?

Put It into Practice

Grab on to God's messaging for the help you need to move
through doubt in order to find the way forward. God will provide you with the tools you need to accomplish your sincere
goals. Know that God is the best co-author of your glorious life
story.

capital letters

Trust in the Lord with all your heart and lean not on your own understanding; in all your ways submit to him, and he will make your paths straight.

PROVERBS 3:5–6 NIV

I am not a good student. Books, math, science, not my thing. Coming from a family of academic overachievers who constantly sailed home with A's as I struggled to drag home C's was more than humiliating. It was debilitating to always be considered the *not-so-bright one.* As I am sure some of you know, the loneliness and isolating disorientation that comes from being lost in a classroom can fill someone with loads of shame. Day in and day out, the frustration from continually trying to just keep up can make you feel...defeated.

When it came time for college, I would just get nauseous. Yes, I would become sick to my stomach and overwhelmed by the thought of my fate. My grades qualified me for not much. One evening as I sat in the living room of my home in Northern Michigan, my mother suggested we get in the car and drive to look at schools as far away as the East Coast, in search of a match. Within days we loaded up the car and off we went.

During our travels we stopped at Cornell University. It seemed my father knew someone who taught there and my mother's mother had gone to Ithaca College, which was located in that same town. My mother had always wanted to visit the campus, so there we were. For me, it was love at first sight. Then, I noticed the hopeless look in my mother's eyes when I told her that this would be a great place for me. I knew full well I was overreaching.

When I attended church back in my hometown that weekend, I prayed hard. We were at the point in the service where we were instructed to lift our private thoughts up to the Lord. And okay, I cheated a bit because I finished my thoughts early. And as the silence continued, I opened my eyes. My gaze drifted and focused on the last word in the program, a word in bold print and in all caps:

CORNELL

CORNELL

It seemed that the man who had walked me to my pew every Sunday of my youth was named *Frank Cornell*. I never knew his name before that day...

CORNELL

I never needed to know it before that day.

At that moment, God filled me with the courage to fight my way in. And fight my way in I did. My path was through the art school. I sent in a portfolio, and the next thing I knew I had secured a personal interview. I was questioned by the head of the Fine Art Department who for some reason took a shine to me. I gained admittance into the less academically demanding College of Art, Architecture, and Planning Fine Arts Department. I later transferred into The College of Arts & Sciences and earned a BA in art history four years later.

The fact that I was one of the first students to graduate from Petoskey High School and go on to an Ivy League school was a miracle.

The fact that I was the first person in my immediate family to graduate from an Ivy League school was a miracle.

The fact that my many years of academic struggles were being rewarded through growing confidence in my abilities, which I discovered at Cornell, was a miracle.

I am here to tell you, Cornell was the perfect place for me. Within months of entering, a perceptive professor recommended that I be tested, diagnosed, and given some concessions for dealing with my learning disabilities. I was treated to many talented professorial lectures and studied shoulder-to-shoulder with numerous bright students, who taught me how to think and learn in ways that were previously unimaginable to me.

I may not have been the brightest, but with the help of God's slight how-to nudge, I landed in a place that allowed my mind to swell.

I know, I know. God doesn't always place into your hand a program with a message in bold print...sometimes He needs you to read the fine print.

Rest assured, no matter which of life's church pews you are sitting in, God is giving you the answers. No, not always in written form. But he will always do it in a way that no matter what your challenges are, you will be able to read and comprehend.

For Further Reflection

When have you walked a path that seemed impossible?
How did God's direction affect your walk?
How was this lofty trail a gift?

Put It into Practice

Release your questions to God and be on the ready to receive direction. Sit, think, push, and move toward where you want to be for it is in the striving that you will be blessed by God's grace, which is wiser and will guide you toward relief from the chains that bind, and into a world of wonder.

a plane

"Have I not commanded you? Be strong and courageous. Do not be frightened, and do not be dismayed, for the Lord your God is with you wherever you go."

JOSHUA 1:9 ESV

My dad was a pilot. He loved to fly. He used to say there was a freedom to flying. He said that, up there, he could go up or down, right or left, whenever and however he wanted to. He found it peaceful when he flew. He claimed he discovered mesmerizing beauty in the air that rivaled anything he had seen on the ground.

When I was in about fifth grade, my dad went in on the purchase of an airplane with two of his friends. They split the costs, like the hangar fees, the airport charges, etc. We would spend weekend afternoons washing the plane, organizing the charts, and pumping up the tires.

My dad had long been enamored with aviation. He grew up in wartime, watching footage of planes with hero pilots emerging from them. It captured his imagination. In college, he enrolled in ROTC in hopes that he would fly for the Navy. But in his senior year, the five-year requirement seemed just too long, so he reluctantly took an assignment on a ship because it had a two-year requirement instead.

When the United States first landed on the moon, my father came home from the office and made everyone gather around the TV to watch. One of our babysitters was there. My father turned to her at one point and said,

"Wouldn't you love to go there and walk around?"

"Oh no, Mr. Brown," she replied. "I am afraid of heights!"

He told that story over and over again. He found it so funny.

But I understood what she meant.

Space, the sky, the clouds, they did not hold the same fascination for me that they did for my dad. Soaring around up there in the backseat of that small, rattly plane scared me. It all made me a bit queasy. Looking out and over the wing at the ground took my breath away. But not in a good way. It was in a more panicky way.

My brain was not like my father's. I did not think like an engineer, the way he did...

On good days

On sunny days

When it was smooth sailing

When he sat in the left seat (that's where the pilot sits; the right seat is reserved for the copilot)

When he sat in the left seat, with his head set on, speaking pilot talk, and I was in the seat behind him and the plane was buzzing and rumbling and humming along...

I would feel safe and calm and so grateful for his aptitude. Those days I felt happy, lucky to follow him up in the air, where I would find animals and faces and flowers and trees in the shadows and in the curves of the clouds.

It was a carefree feeling.

It was a weightless feeling.

It was a heavenly feeling.

In those moments, I was not scared of heights like my babysitter was.

In those moments, I felt anything was possible.

In those moments, I felt if we went up up up, who knows what kind of wonderful we might find.

But when the bumps came and when the rain fell, when lightning sparked and flashed in the distance, I would get scared for him. I would get scared for me, for my sisters, brother, and mother. I would clutch the seat. I would hold my breath, and I would pray. Oh...the promises I made to the Good Lord above. Oh...the deals I made.

But when the weather started to roar, my dad's love of flying soared. He was a great pilot. Approximately 50 percent of all pilots get their instrument ratings, but only 15 percent keep their ratings current. Dad logged in enough hours, received enough instruction, to get his instrument rating. That meant he could fly under instrument rules, or for those in the know, IFR. In other words, he could fly in the toughest conditions. My dad loved the challenges that came with turbulence and storms.

He explained it like this: You file your instrument flight plan with air traffic control when you want to go up in treacherous weather. When you do, it allows you to have a preplanned route through the air that is only for you. For example, when there is so much cloud cover that you cannot see what is in front of you or below you, that is the moment in flying when you really have to have faith in your instruments. That is the moment you can no longer rely on your senses. Those instruments, and the electricity you cannot see that informs them, is all you can rely on. In those moments, the mechanics of it—the combination of fuel and electronics and engineering—were a marvel to him.

They were a marvel to me, too, but in quite a different way. To me it would be a mysterious marvel, something I could never really grasp. When my head was in those clouds, charging through foul weather, I went through a myriad of emotions: fear, worry, suspense. My body would fill with tension and I would experience the most catastrophic thinking. Then the plane would start to *beep beep beep*. The clouds would clear, signaling that the runway was near. Moments before we would land, I could see the ground and I would begin to breathe again.

Alleluia, I would think.

Simultaneously, those were the only moments when my dad would say that being a pilot could become demanding. "During the landing," he explained, "is when you have to work with air traffic control. It's when you have to focus on the runway lights. It's when you have to rely on your own depth perception to spot and judge your relationship to other planes." My dad never broke a sweat when he flew. He used to tell me, "You do not panic in a car; well, flying is just like riding in a car. You know the car will do what it is supposed to do. A plane is just as reliable. You trust your car and you should trust our plane." It seemed so obviously logical to him.

He valued that the view up there showed you a world that was unperceivable when you walked the earth: the checkerboard landscapes, the snaking shapes of the rivers, the perfect roundness of lakes and ponds, and the tops of trees. Dad said that nighttime, especially when flying in the western sky, over very few towns, caused an endless blackness that was breathtaking.

When we touched down no matter what the weather, he would calmly unload us all out of the cramped plane, pile us into the car, and head for home.

On the ride home, I would run through my head all the different possible endings to our flight we could have experienced. I would wonder if my father ever did this. If he ever prayed to God as the wind blew and the plane bumped around. Or if he just knew he had the instruments and skills to get us through almost any weather the atmosphere brought our way.

I realized then that faith was an individual thing. It's a morphable thing. Tailored to the individual soul. God is an adept engineer who knows what your instrument rating is at any given time.

Sometimes you have to rely solely on God's guidance because you cannot see your way through the storm. Sometimes God will provide you with a view that will get you through. Sometimes you might have to lean into your skills—along with GOD's grace—in order to land you right where you need to be.

I am afraid of heights. I believe we are all afraid of something. Even my confident father, with mad flying skills, recognized that extreme weather conditions would keep him from flying.

I humbly ask you, please hold on to the belief that those phony heights, those fake fears, can be conquered when you trust and believe in God as your pilot in the LEFT seat as you sit in the RIGHT seat—you're a cooperating copilot.

Be in the RIGHT seat so that you can be handed the instruments you need to get to where you have to go.

For Further Reflection

When have you trusted, and when have you been frightened?
How did God help you through your fear?
How was your trust a gift?

Put It into Practice

Trust that God will be there to navigate you through all the storms that you will fly through. Believe that God knows when to take you up into the weather and when to allow you to land on sunny shores.

a drink

And Jacob was left alone. And a man wrestled with him until the breaking of the day.

GENESIS 32:24 ESV

Wine, margaritas, beer, gin and tonics, sangria, rum punches are all my friends. Or maybe I should really say they are all my frenemies. Me and drinking have always had a thing. We have always had a love-hate relationship.

My mother and father were both teetotalers. Why? Well, they had reasons. First, my mother had an alcoholic father. My dad grew up hearing tales of his alcoholic grandfather. They both believed that there was a good chance that alcoholism is genetic. They believed that they and their children were at greater risk to become alcoholics. More than that, they loved life and felt grateful to be on this earth. They couldn't understand why anyone would want to alter the experience of living for even one single moment of the day.

These lines were at least part of the song I heard in my head whenever I reached for a mood-altering beverage.

The other chorus was from way down deep—deep down in my being. It was a need to get out of myself. A need to move beyond the limits of comfort. Many who do not know me well will find it hard to believe I am shy. Truly, without the aid of alcohol, I am not sure I could have sat through many past conversations or parties, or accomplished many of the things I have because I was just too riddled with self-doubt.

In the quest to get creative and dig deeper, I often turned to the aid of a few drinks. Under their influence, I would often find myself drifting into a creative place that I might never have stumbled upon without the loosening effects of alcohol. Time and time again I find I need to be awakened from a mood that is not serving me well or those around me. When I down a drink, things seem a bit brighter and lighter.

I know.

I know.

These are all fairly typical reasons to indulge in the sauce. I feel my motivations are sincere, helpful, useful, even practical. I believe that, for the most part, drinking has served me well.

I have a dear uncle. His name is Moey, short for Moses. Yep, it's biblical, which makes perfect sense to me. He was the patriarch of our rather large family. He was the quiet warrior who selflessly gave to his community and to our clan. Every time he wrote me a letter, he signed it: *Go to Church and do not drink beer.* When I would take my leave after visiting him, his departing phrase was always, "Drop the bottle."

You guessed it. He, like my folks, was a nondrinker.

I had grown up watching my grown-ups reject cocktail hour.

When it came time to make my own decision, I dug in. Sometimes I would do so lightly. Other times, I would go deep.

When I was in my twenties, I was in an off-off-Broadway play. I played a drunk. While my character was under the influence, she drove a busload of kids into a tree. One small child on the bus died.

To prepare for that role, I spent time in AA meetings in some of the roughest corners of the Lower East Side of Manhattan. I heard excruciating accounts of the role alcohol had played in the destruction of people's lives.

I went through periods of abstinence and periods when I was a daily drinker. Me and alcohol, we had a relationship. Sometimes we were talking and sometimes we were fighting. I knew that I was genetically disposed to be a victim of alcoholism. So, gingerly I have treaded, always checking in with myself and others to see if the drink was taking over or if I was still getting something out of my relationship with it. I never thought of it as right or wrong, black or white. Rather, the whole issue has been something gray and cloudy—a line I had to walk carefully.

It seems our country also grapples with the issue of consumption. Prohibition in the United States was a nationwide constitutional ban on alcoholic beverages from 1920 to 1933. On March 21, 1933, FDR signed into law the Cullen-Harrison Act, legalizing beer and wine with an alcohol content of 3.2 percent or less. However, it took another eight months for the Twenty-first Amendment to be ratified, ending Prohibition for good on December 5, 1933.

The question of the legal drinking age shifts from eighteen to twenty-one, depending on where, when, and what state of the union you come of age in.

As I write this book, I am witness to the Kavanaugh confirmation hearings, where some of the debate centers around the consequences and accountability of underage drinking.

I cannot tell you how many times I have prayed for clarity.

Then I began raising children of my own. *Please, God, guide me in how and when and if I should partake.* I get that this is not the most crucial discourse to call upon God to participate in, because for me, it is a choice I am making rather than a condition or situation I find myself in. However, in my life's journey, it seems to be a constant concerning thread when determining how to live my life.

I was engaged in a wrestling match. When I look to the Bible . . . it, too, sends conflicting directions. Ecclesiastes 9:7 says, "Go, eat your food with gladness, and drink your wine with a joyful heart, for God has already approved what you do" (NIV). While Ephesians 5:18 says, "Do not get drunk on wine, which leads to debauchery. Instead, be filled with the Spirit" (NIV).

I also looked to the Book of Genesis, to the story of God calling on Jacob to wrestle with Him. God answered Jacob by requiring him to wrestle with Him *all* night long. God did not simply speak to Jacob in a dream or a vision as He had at other times; He engaged him in combat.

I take stock in this strange wrestling match. That God's answers sometimes arrive only after many seasons of battle.

My season came when menopause arrived at my doorstep. Oh, how I wanted to ignore it. I wanted to be that woman who barely skips a beat when this change of life came. I wanted to be the warrior princess who could soldier on through the battle against time. So I grabbed my weapon of choice. I suited up by tossing back cocktail after cocktail, hoping it would suppress the onslaught of physical and emotional changes I was experiencing.

But each full glass of wine I downed only accentuated my despair. The liquor seemed to add fuel to my fiery hormones. After many sleepless nights and tender mornings, it occurred to me that perhaps drinking always had exacerbated whatever I was trying to muscle through. Perhaps now I was just wise enough to know the difference.

My battle came to an end when God's natural timing forced

me to stop. God dealt me a final blow I could not rise above. God forced my worn-out will to sit with all my discomfort long enough to discover the peace and growth that came with the acceptance of who and where I really was. My crutch, my go-to habit of indulgence, was no longer there to help me look the other way. I was present and I needed to be in order to walk through this fire toward my next act.

No matter what you are grappling with...

No matter what you are struggling with...

No matter what clarity you are yearning for...

Stay engaged with God even if He shows up looking like your adversary by withholding what you are wanting in the moment. Stay engaged in the battle. Because sometimes it is during the struggle, with fists drawn, with your mind on high alert season after season, that God's light will eventually shine bright enough to bring your query to an end.

For Further Reflection

Where in your life do you have a continuing battle for clarity?

How do you stay engaged in your quest for clarity?

How is God involved in the conflict that has gone unresolved in your life?

How has this extended quest for direction been a gift?

Put It into Practice

Stay in the question at the heart of your struggle. Be diligent in your query no matter how disconcerting it may be to live in that uncertainty. If you stay engaged, the struggle itself could be a benefit.

a cold

Do not be anxious about anything, but in every situation, by prayer and petition, with thanksgiving, present your requests to God.

PHILIPPIANS 4:6 NIV

We were lucky enough to meet our adopted daughter, Meredith, just a few days after she was born. I felt so happy to be with her from the moment she came into this world. We would have been there on day one to greet her, but our little love bug was born weeks earlier than she was supposed to. I rarely left Meredith while she spent a scary spell in an incubator in the NICU. Thankfully, within a week or so, our Meredith was thriving and ready to make the trip from her home state of Ohio to our home state of New York.

Meredith was mine and I was hers.

Soon after we brought her home, Meredith got sick. It seemed to be just a cold. I was a bit concerned it might be more serious. Even my five-year-old daughter, Prentiss, was worried. "Mom," she asked, "why does our brown baby look white?"

Prentiss was right. Meredith's light brown skin was awfully pale. The nurses in the NICU told me that most babies of color will have changes in skin tone during the first few months of their life. However, they told me it would get darker, not lighter. Also, our beautiful bundle had become rather listless. Now, it was true that I believed she had a mellow nature, but I was just getting to know her, so my take on her temperament could have been off.

I was grateful we had a doctor's appointment the next day for a weigh-in and checkup—a perfect opportunity to put my fears to rest. When we arrived at our pediatrician's office, my Meredith seemed to have grown paler and quieter. I was nervous. The doctor examined her, listening to her heart and her breathing. She looked in her mouth and in her ears. She finished her onceover, and declared that she felt Meredith was just badly congested. The doctor was quite sure it would clear up on its own.

I felt uneasy with that diagnosis. It just was not sitting well with me. Over the previous twenty-four hours I had become increasingly concerned. "I am surprised," I responded. "I really thought when we got here that you were going to send us directly to the hospital." With that the doctor gently pressed her stethoscope against Meredith's back. Seconds later, she shot up, went to her phone, and dialed a number.

Minutes later there was an ambulance waiting for us outside the doctor's office. The next thing I knew, Meredith and I were being rushed through the streets of New York, sirens blaring. At the hospital we were greeted with a giant hospital bed on wheels. My barely born Meredith was loaded on it. She looked so small lying there, the bed seeming to swallow her up. I stayed next to her side while she was rolled into a harshly lit room. There, a swarm of hospital personnel surrounded her.

One doctor popped out of the hive and walked my way. In an urgent tone he said, "We need to intubate your daughter."

"NO," I blurted out.

"Perhaps you don't understand," he said, "but your baby needs help breathing."

"NO," I repeated sternly.

The hive regrouped to discuss, and agreed to try other less drastic measures. *Phew*, I thought. You see, I had just been with my father in intensive care, where he was put on a breathing machine. As a result of that, he developed an infection that placed him in more danger than his original illness. He was close to death from the intubation procedure. I was not about to have that same thing happen to my child.

Meredith was mine and I was hers.

They had our pediatrician call me. "Katie," she said, "they must intubate Meredith."

"NO," was my response.

They asked if it was due to religious concerns.

"NO," was my frustrated answer, "but if that makes it easier for you to understand and find another solution, then YES."

By now my husband had arrived. After he had huddled with the experts, he calmly told me that Meredith could die if we did not agree to this intubation.

I stared long and hard at my baby. She lay there with tubes and needles attached to seemingly every part of her. She seemed even smaller and more helpless than when we first entered this cold room. Her head was completely wrapped in gauze and her sparkly little eyes struggled to stay open.

I loved her so.

I closed my eyes, plugged my nose, and relented.

Meredith was diagnosed with RSV, respiratory syncytial

virus. RSV is a common virus that infects the respiratory tract. And though most cases cause nothing more than a cold, premature babies are at greater risk of the virus developing into an infection that can cause serious problems and can even become life-threatening.

Meredith, with her head wrapped and breathing with the aid of a machine, was wheeled to a private room so as not to infect others. Our minster and his wife, Terri, were our first visitors on that dark day in that massive hospital with our small struggling baby.

Terri, who I had grown to know and love, stretched out her hand to mine just minutes after she arrived. I held on tight and whimpered, "I do not know if I can do this," as we gazed down at my needy child. She squeezed my hand harder, looked me straight in the eye, and without missing a beat, confidently said, "You can, you will, and you must be strong enough for this. Meredith," she emphasized, "needs you."

Yep yep yep, Meredith needed me. *Yes, I can, and we will get through this*, I thought.

Too many agonizing days later to count, we brought our girl home again. The whole ordeal made me realize that I needed to be better prepared when and if Meredith had another medical emergency. Our trusted pediatrician suggested I learn all I could about her "family's" health history. Which would also help me be better prepared if she needed me to explain where her parents and people were from. I'd be better prepared if she needed clarity concerning her heritage in order to find her sense of place in the world. At the same time, this frightening experience made me realize what a fierce protective love I had for my Meredith. That strong motherly love made me want to bury my head in the sand. Because I loved her so much, I needed her to be mine so much, that it made me afraid of the answers I may find. I was afraid that: *If I got educated, if we found out about her people, would it make her less ours, less mine? I know, I know. Really, I mean who cares. But somehow I did care. I never wanted Meredith to be part of any family but mine. I am ashamed to admit that it seemed an infantile emotion had developed along with my new role of being an adoptive mother. These were not my noblest thoughts. I was jealous. This infantile part of me wanted to keep quiet, keep us all in the dark to ensure we could keep Meredith all to ourselves. I knew these were not noble thoughts. I was not proud.*

Meredith was mine and I was hers.

My pediatrician gave me the number of someone who, she believed, was one of the most esteemed geneticists of our time. So I did it. I forced myself to be bigger than my chidlish need *never* to acknowledge that she was part of any other family but ours. I took a deep breath and scheduled an appointment.

The day had come, and as we were being ushered into the examination room, I found myself getting choked up. I tried to push away the feeling that I wanted Meredith's history to be my history. My insecurities as a mother wanted her to need and know only me and us. I am ashamed to say I was really struggling.

Then the doctor walked into the room. She looked like a young Jane Goodall. If you were casting a top geneticist, and you needed to cast someone who seemed sympathetic and wise, you would cast this woman. "How can I help you?" she asked in a tender voice, sensing my trepidation.

"Meredith is adopted," I blurted out, my voice cracking. *Pull it together, Katie,* I thought. "I was hoping you could tell me what her racial makeup is. We do not know if Meredith is African or

Hispanic. Meredith's mother was white, but we do not know anything about her father. We want to know so that we can supplement her health record history. So I may help her settle," I continued, "any uncertainty she may suffer due to not knowing."

I took a deep and emotional breath. *Help me, God. I am feeling a bit embarrassed. Please, God, do not let her recognize my fear.* At that moment, a Scripture from Galatians flashed through my mind: "There is neither Jew nor Greek, there is neither slave nor free, there is no male and female, for you are all one in Christ Jesus" (3:28 ESV).

My Jane Goodall responded with a sigh, "I am not sure you are asking the right question." She then placed her hand on mine and said, "Meredith is more like you than not. Ninety-nine percent of her genetic makeup is identical to yours." She continued, "We have learned that all humans are closely related. We all have the same collection of genes. We have developed a sort of family tree of humans that reveals all people alive today are Africans. So that should answer part of your question. The variations in people's skin color has to do with proximity to the sun. So, what I can do is tell you the region of the world your daughter's tribe is from. But know that her race, your race, are the same. The differences between your genetic makeup and hers are simple and minuscule."

Meredith was mine and I was hers.

I felt a sense of calm as I embraced her soothing news. Yes. Yes. Of course I already knew about the broad strokes she had laid out for me concerning genetic makeup. But somehow, as a rookie adoptive mama of my beautiful Meredith, I needed a hand in getting past my jealousy of her birth family.

This dear doctor had just reassured me that Meredith, at her core, was like our family and me, and we were like her. She was a part of us and we were a part of her long before that day. I chuckled as I thought, *I went that day to define what made her different and her people different from us. Instead, I was treated to an education in what made us the same.*

Now, I know this all seems terribly obvious. In this day and age, we all know that we are part of one big human family. Right?

For some reason, for me, being an adoptive mother meant that I needed to hear that our differences were only skin deep. It was humbling to admit that even I, a progressive, was jealous and insecure about whether my Meredith would understand that my love and familiarity toward her was grounded in a deep reality that was as legitimate as the similarities she would have with her birth family.

Only God could have been the one to orchestrate a way to reassure me right then and there when I needed it most, and from the expert of all experts. God embraced my petty insecurities and matched them with a slam-dunk move to assure me.

God's mercy did not judge me for my need to hear again what I already understood. God knew how high the stakes were for me. God paired me with an expert spokesperson, who blessed me with her empathy. Who laid out, with tender sympathy, the obvious blessing: I already had all I needed to be a "REAL MOTHER" to my Meredith.

Never be afraid to say out loud to God your genuine, foolish fears. Never be afraid to share with God your heartfelt idiotic immaturity. Because if you are truly honest with God, you will find that God will uplift you and your shortcomings with the holy intel to help you walk onward and upward.

For Further Reflection

When have you moved on from an embarrassing fear?
How did God's grace exist in this experience?
How was this fear a gift?

Put It into Practice

Admit to God any of your thoughts and fears that do not make you proud. Then release them into God's very capable hands.

Norman Rockwell

I sought the Lord, and he answered me; he delivered me from all my fears.

PSALM 34:4 NIV

I woke up this morning and found myself at a complete loss. We were on vacation on the Long Island Sound in a little beach shack. I thought if I went there, I would be moved to write, write, write! I had got in late the night before. When I awoke, I was feeling guilty. Feeling like I had indulged myself with this vacation before my book was even finished, and before a lot of other pressing work was completed.

To make matters worse, I had forgotten my computer. What a loser. I came here to write and had nothing to write with. Without my laptop, I could not even access my list of stories that I still had left to write. My mind was blank and my heart was sick.

So . . . I started this morning like I do every morning with a conversation with God:

I am here.
I hope I did the right thing.
I am feeling anxious that I should not have taken this trip.
But now here I am, and I can hardly remember stories I need to write.

My mind seems to be blank and I am feeling homesick and not good
about myself.
Help me. If You can.
I need to know what I am supposed to do and if I am in the right place
and doing the right thing.
Please?
I love You, God.
I just want to do right by You.
Amen.

With that, I opened my eyes and tiptoed down the stairs since everyone else was asleep. I did not want to wake them. I was kind of curious to see the place. I had come in too late the night before to have a good look-see. The first thing I saw was a giant window at the bottom of the stairs. In the corner of that window, right at the bottom of the stairs, right in front of me, the name "Norman Rockwell" was written.

My heart leapt. You see, I have a story about Norman Rockwell and me. Mr. Rockwell was even the subject of one of my stories. As I walked into the center of the room, and gazed out the window, I could see that the window framed one of the loveliest views of the shoreline and neighboring cottages. It was obviously the owners' intent, by placing the artist's signature in the lower-left-hand corner, to imply that the view was as pretty as a painting. The fact that the artist they chose was none other than MY Norman Rockwell ... well, all I can say is that I knew what I would be writing about that day.

Amen. Thank You, God.

I felt right again. I felt like I could again. I was not alone.

My Norman Rockwell story goes like this:

I had applied to Cornell University. A stretch school for me, for sure, especially because my GPA was below what they accepted. Cornell was a place I could see myself really digging into. I especially loved their bohemian and interesting art school. Art was definitely my favorite subject, by far. My parents had fostered in my siblings and me a real love for art. They cultivated in us an admiration for the artists themselves—for their work and their important voice in the world.

Somehow, I managed to land an interview with the dean of the art school. I had to try, and with an interview, maybe, just maybe, somehow, I could talk my way in. Maybe, with some kind of a miracle, my love of all things art would be my ticket.

When they gave me the meeting place and time, they also asked me to bring my portfolio.

A portfolio?
What is a portfolio?
Got it. Got it. Got it.
A collection of my artwork.
Okay, done.
All in one big pile.
Ready to roll.

At that moment my art teacher intervened. She had big bold hair and still wore bell bottoms in the eighties. She was my most supportive teacher ever. And this day was no exception. She walked to her closet and came back with a rather large black-leather-envelope-type case complete with handles and a zipper that went almost all around it.

Correction...NOW I was ready to roll.

I settled into a chair in the dean's office at Cornell University. A portly, tad disheveled, eccentric man sat across from me. It was a friendly enough conversation. Where was I from? What were my art classes like? What medium did I like best: charcoal, water color, oils? "You name it, I liked it all," was my reply. I was getting my groove. *I got this*, I thought. Still nervous, though, I continued to plow ahead in a seemingly confident way. Next question? Who is my favorite artist?

My favorite artist?
My heart stopped.
Artist?
Artist?
Who was my favorite artist?
I did not remember the names of any artist.
Why?
All the museums I had been to.
All the art hanging in my house.
All the discussions about artists.
Nothing?
I got nothing.
My mind went blank.
My heart started racing faster.
How could I not remember the names of any artists?
Artist? Artist? Artist?
My palms were sweaty. I looked down and around anything?
Anything?
Artist?
Who was my favorite artist?
Help me, God.

Do not let me blow this.
Then it came to me ...

A week earlier, an Arby's had opened in my hometown. It was big news. It was the first fast-food restaurant in the county, complete with a drive-through. It was thrilling. Oh, how I loved their ham and cheese sandwiches. They were hot, gooey, and delicious. When you bought a drink there, you were given your beverage in a glass that had the painting of a famous artist on it. There were four different paintings featured on a set of four glasses. I so wanted to collect all four. The first and only glass I had gotten at that point was one of an artist with a pipe in his mouth seated at a canvas, looking off to the side at his subject.

But who was that artist? Yes! I can see the painting. But who was the artist? Help me out, God. What is the name of that artist? THEN, It came to me: Norman Rockwell.

"Norman Rockwell is my favorite artist," I proclaimed. *Phew*, I thought. "Yep! Norman Rockwell!" I stated again boldly.

There was a long pause. "Who?" he asked.

I felt like his tone was almost daring me to repeat myself.

Ah, he's impressed, I thought.

So, I sat a little taller and said even louder, "Norman Rockwell."

The dean sat back in his chair. "Really?"

"Yep. Norman Rockwell," I repeated.

There was silence. Clearly he was contemplating the brilliance of my response. "And why is he your favorite artist?" he asked.

OH DEAR Help me, God. "WELLLLL ... I feel his characterization of American life was very celebratory," I answered. Where that came from, I have no idea.

Thank You God, I thought.

He replied rather sternly, "YES, that is why many of us, in the art world, feel he is an illustrator and NOT an artist."

"WELLL…I disagree. I think any painter who can evoke a feeling, of any sort in anyone, is an artist; and for me, Norman makes me feel right at home."

Norman! Norman? Was I on a first-name basis with the man?

After another long pause, he said, "Would you like to see my art?"

"Yes, please," I replied.

He pointed to the wall behind me. Hanging there were a series of photos of what looked like cloud formations in the sky. He explained he flies a plane that lets out a massive amount of smoke. He then draws with that smoke as he rolls and spins.

He pilots the plane just so, in order to create these large designs in the sky while someone on the ground photographs them.

I was perplexed and found myself almost speechless. Why would anyone make art that would be so impermanent, so fleeting, so untraditional?

"Thank you so much for coming in and sharing your work with me, Katie," he said as he ushered me out the door. "Norman Rockwell," he muttered under his breath, but just loud enough for me to hear.

I did attend the College of Art, Architecture, and Planning Fine Arts Department at Cornell. I do think that eccentric dean had a hand in getting me in. I think he was so perplexed, surprised, and concerned that someone would be so naïve. So stunned that someone who dreamed of being an artist in the early eighties would consider Norman Rockwell their favorite artist. I think he felt he and the school had to take me under their wing.

To this day, I believe if my answer had been Picasso, Monet, or Rembrandt, I would have blended in as just another applicant. The series of blessings that brought me to that room, in that way, with that man made me believe in the phrase "a match made in heaven"—the naïve Midwestern want-to-be art student meets Cornell University's avant-garde fine arts dean.

By the way, when I finally did reunite with my laptop? It turns out my Norman Rockwell tale was not even on the list!

For Further Reflection

When was there surprising strength in your unpreparedness? How was God able to enhance this impromptu moment? How was your naïveté a gift?

Put It into Practice

Know that the unexpected, the unknown, the unready is sometimes more than enough for God to move you forward. God knows what you need to know to maneuver you through life. God arms you with the right stuff at the right time—always.

HURT

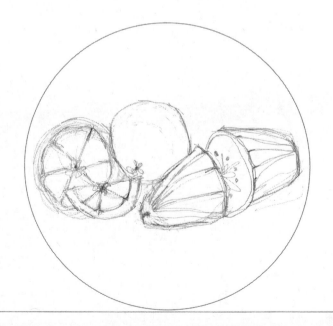

a drive by

Therefore, as God's chosen people, holy and dearly loved, clothe yourselves with compassion, kindness, humility, gentleness and patience.

COLOSSIANS 3:12 NIV

I was shot in a drive-by shooting, with a .38 caliber pistol. It still seems unbelievable to say.

In my late twenties, I was walking down a street in Los Angeles, at dusk, when out of nowhere, one shot was fired. That bullet entered the back of my leg directly behind my knee.

Time seemed to slow in the moments that followed.

I remember screaming at the top of my lungs.

I remember a burning sensation.

I remember the sound was so subtle, almost like a firecracker going off.

I remember feeling the warmth of the blood against my skin.

I remember screaming at the top of my lungs, but barely hearing it.

I remember that the scene seemed chaotic, but my mind was calm.

I thought, *I have had such a good life. I love my family. I was a fast skier* (yep, I really thought that). I felt a sensation that was warm and safe and happy. I felt like I was outside of my body and looking on with silent satisfaction. All the while, I was begging for help, hysterically calling for someone to save me.

The next thing I knew, a red beat-up four-door hatchback pulled up on the sidewalk. A panicked African-American man jumped out of the driver's seat, took off his jacket, and tied it around my leg to try to stop the bleeding. He lifted me in the backseat of what was an extremely messy car. He held my leg up high as he drove us through the streets of LA to a hospital. When we stopped outside the ER, he ran in and grabbed a wheelchair. Moving fast, he once again lifted me and placed me into the chair and wheeled me through the swinging doors. The woman behind the desk was demanding insurance as my warrior said, "She already told you she does not have any. Now let her see a doctor!"

I could see that kind man's face in the round window of the examination room until the doctor came to my bedside . . . and then he was gone and I never saw him again.

Several surgeries and months later, I was still struggling on the road to recovery without health insurance and without a job. The pain from that bullet during my recovery took me to some dark and venomous places. I remember many nights as I lay alone, closing my eyes tightly and imagining that I was holding a gun to my assailant's head and slowly pulling the trigger. I awoke sweating night after night from a piercing popping sound in my head. I would sit up straight in my bed as my body relived the moment of impact. On those rare occasions in between surgeries, when I was able to go out into the world, I would walk hunched over, trying to protect my head, for it seemed far too vulnerable.

According to my doctors and therapist, I was suffering from post-traumatic shock syndrome. Somehow that diagnosis served as a wake-up call to my self-absorbed twenty-something self. It made me think of all the soldiers whose daily routine is rapid fire. I felt humbled and humiliated that I had experienced only one shot, one bullet.

As I became more desperate to pay my mounting hospital bills, I thought about how, at one moment in time, I had found myself at the wrong place at the wrong time, and how that had introduced overwhelming turbulence and violence into my life. I thought that if my privileged life had become so quickly damaged, how easy it would be to dismantle and therefore cause dire desperation in the lives of those less fortunate.

I was in yet another hospital for yet another surgery, in excruciating pain. I found myself closing my eyes so tightly and replacing the gun I had imagined so many times in my hand with a hazy image of me pouring a healing yellow light all over my perpetrator's body. Night after night as I slowly embraced the recurring picture of that comforting light, the image became less hazy. The glow of that yellow light became brighter and brighter. It came more into focus as the nights wore on. Soon, I looked forward to closing my eyes just to catch a glimpse of that healing image.

As I lay there in the hospital bed, it occurred to me that while that bullet caused me to experience the worst of humanity, it also delivered to me the best of humanity with the arrival of my hero/ angel in a red hatchback car.

Two police officers visited my bedside. They questioned me about the shooting incident. They then asked me if I would fill out some paperwork they would leave behind for me. We exchanged pleasant good-byes and they said they would be by to pick up the papers the next day.

As I muddled through the fill-in-the-blank questionnaire, I

began to pay attention to the fine print. There, buried in the bottom, was a section marked "Victims of Violent Crimes." This section laid out a California program covering all medical costs for those who had been victimized. A plan, I heard, that was partially funded by parking violation payments. Needless to say, I now pay my parking tickets with...pleasure. From there on out, all bills, past and present, were sent to and paid for by the great state of California's Restitution Program!

To say that bullet filled me up with the great gift of compassion and a deep understanding of the phrase "there but for the grace of God go I" is an understatement.

To say that the bullet made me tune into human suffering in a way that I could never have done without the pain and the loneliness of being victimized is an understatement.

And all the while, no matter how dark the night, I always felt God's healing hand trying to pull me up and over my anger and grief so that I could see the light.

So, when I had truly tuned into the how-to that life's evil bullet provided, that is when God provided me with the fine print of how to settle the bill and walk toward the light.

For Further Reflection

How has the occurrence of a physical hurt changed you, shifted your perspective, or opened up your heart?

How has God met you during your healing process and moved in a different direction?

How has your new view or level of understanding been a gift?

Put It into Practice

Find the spiritual healing within physical hurt. Remember to rehab your heart and mind. Pay attention to where your negative thoughts are taking you on your road to recovery because sometimes it is in that grief-stricken thinking that you will find your redemption.

a comment

Opening his mouth, Peter said: "I most certainly understand now that God is not one to show partiality."

ACTS 10:34–35 NASB

There she was, standing right in front of me. When I walked into the little washroom that stood between me and the room full of newborns, I almost bumped into her. I knew it was her the minute I saw her. She was the birth mother. She was my newborn adopted baby's birth mother.

She was my Meredith's birth mother. She was small and lovely, and we both fell into each other's arms without saying a word. She then guided me over to the sink and waited patiently as I washed my hands. The running water was warm, and it was the only sound that broke the silence as we both took each other in with the compassion that only two women who were total strangers yet meant so much to each other could. I cannot really remember the first minute I saw Meredith, but I will never forget the moment I saw Misty.

She was my angel.

She was quite short.

She was so generous.

She was whiter than me.

She seemed so sure of herself.

I felt so inadequate.

She was Meredith's Mother.

I wanted to become Meredith's Mother.

We walked shoulder to shoulder through the door and into the neonatal intensive care unit. I then followed her until she stopped next to an incubator right in the middle of a row of incubators. There was my little lady, behind the glass of the incubator, looking so small, helpless, and peaceful. A few nurses were nearby, and Misty's mother, Meredith's birth grandmother, who was fierce and determined. She told me how proud she was of her daughter for making this decision. She said it was the most unselfish decision her Misty had ever made.

Man!

I hoped I would not let them down. I hoped I could love Meredith with that same kind of unconditional selfless love that her birth mother did.

I learned about the possibility of Meredith just a month earlier. From there, things moved quickly. My husband and I were thrilled and somewhat stunned that this all came true. Were we really there holding our new baby in our hands? It felt so right.

I am ashamed to say I was hesitant when my husband had suggested we adopt. I wondered if I could love a baby who did not come from my belly as much as I loved one who did. You see, my heart busted with love for my baby daughter, Prentiss, whom I had given birth to five years earlier. I would do anything to keep her safe. That I knew for sure. Would I have that same motherly instinct toward an adopted baby? I certainly hoped so, but I must admit in the back of my thoughts I wondered. My superb husband thought my fears were absurd. His confidence allowed me to march on.

So here we were...holding a bundle of love that seemed so pure and so perfect and so all that. She was more than I could have ever thought possible. Yes, she was born premature, but she was five pounds, a giant compared to the three-pound premature baby girl Prentiss I had given birth to. The doctors insisted that Meredith stay in the NICU until they were sure all was well.

I stayed with her around the clock. Sometimes, I think it was for me more than for her. I felt I needed to earn the right to be her mother, and my presence was the first step in getting there.

It was sheer bliss to hold her tight, skin to skin, while smelling her head and counting her fingers and toes. How did I get so lucky? How could I make her understand how blessed I felt to be chosen to be her mom? Oh, how I hoped I would be enough.

The only moments I left her was when the nurses needed to conduct a test or reattach her feeding tubes.

I found this particularly difficult because I felt so inadequate, knowing that I could not feed her. I felt so sad that I would not be able to breastfeed Meredith like I thought most good and true mothers did, like I had been able to do with my Prentiss.

I was so very grateful for these nurses. I was sure they sensed my heartache because they taught me how to hold her as she was being fed through a tube and eventually how to fill her bottles and get her little self to drink. I was particularly fond of one nurse who seemed to spend the most time with my Meredith. It probably also helped that she was a fan of my TV show.

In the wee hours of the morning, she would tell me how great she thought all my recipes were. One such morning, at about 3:00 a.m., she returned my Meredith to my arms after she'd walked her through a flurry of activity. As I held Meredith close, my favorite nurse sat down next to me and said..."You know your baby is black?"

"What?"

"Do you know your baby is black?"

I sat up straighter and held Meredith tighter. "Yes, I do. But why would you ask that?"

"Well," she said, "I just thought someone like you would like to have the perfect family."

My jaw stiffened as I said, "I do have the perfect family. And Meredith makes my family perfect."

In that moment I stood up. I stood up with all the might of a lioness who was ready to do anything to protect her cub.

In that moment I felt the rage that only a mother would know and feel deep down in her bones.

In that moment I realized Meredith would grow up in a world different from mine.

In that moment I felt the sting of racism in a way that felt deeply personal.

In that moment I knew I was Meredith's mother.

It did not take God long to reach me, right there in the wee hours of the dark night, while I sat stunned with a deeply flawed caregiver.

Right there, God turned the light on just long enough for me to snap to and feel deeply the motherly bond that I had with my Meredith.

Right there, at a very dark moment of stark realization, God reached out and turned my outrage into relief that I could and would be Meredith's mother.

I turned my back to this woman and sang *my* daughter to sleep.

For Further Reflection

When have you been stung by judgment that in turn served
you well?

How did God lead you through this experience?

How did that offense become a gift?

Put It into Practice

Confront evil with faith in order to recapture a Godly love that
will bring you a deeper perspective.

a movie

For by grace you have been saved through faith. And this is not your own doing; it is the gift of God.

EPHESIANS 2:8 ESV

We had lost a child. We had lost a child before it came to term. It was early on in the pregnancy, but so devastating. I felt it was my fault. I agonized for so many reasons, but the biggest reason was that I felt I did not take good care. I was filled with remorse because I should have done better. I was convinced the blame was mine.

I spent most of that day in my bed unable to move from the excruciating pain physically and emotionally. How had I found myself here?

I tried to sleep but could not. So, I channel-surfed, trying to find a movie that looked like it would fit my mood. I happened upon *Places in the Heart*, a movie that had come out years earlier. The movie begins with the hymn "Blessed Assurance" playing as the viewers see a church service ending in the distance. Then the movie rolls into a series of vignettes that introduce us to the characters and places we are about to see. The movie takes place in 1935 in Waxahachie, Texas, during the heart of the Depression. It is a gut-wrenching story of a widow, played by Sally Field, who fights with all she has and never knew she had to keep her farm and her family intact.

The story unfolds and twists and turns and drags your heart along with every inch that passes. This was perfect for me and my state of being. It was relentless in its struggles, yet there were glimmers of hope. The good, the bad, the ugly that is human spilled out in each frame.

Then came the ending! It hit me so hard. The last scene of the movie jumped from fantasy to reality by showing the image of the man sitting in a church pew who had been killed handing a church communion plate to the boy who killed him. This movie was brutal in its accuracy of the portrait it created of the turmoil of the time. Yet it broke my feelings wide open when it portrayed this final hopeful vision.

"It was an attempt at reconciliation between the characters. There are certain things images can explain and words cannot," said Robert Benton, writer-director of *Places in the Heart*, in an interview with the *New York Times* while explaining why he ended his extremely realistic movie with the wish-fulfillment fantasy of two dead men sharing the body and blood of Christ in a communion service. He said, "There is something in the image of the man who has been killed handing the communion plate to the boy who killed him that seems very moving to me in ways I cannot explain. I had the ending before I ever finished the screenplay. Although, I knew audiences would be confused about it."

It was late at night and I was beat up and tired. I shut the TV off and laid my head on the pillow. I was hoping the roller-coaster ride the movie had taken me on would leave me exhausted enough to drift off and not dwell on my real life despair. For a bit at least, I believe I slept, but I was awakened by an image that rocked me to my core: the image was of me seated in a church pew...with babies at various stages of development seated right next to me.

I woke up in a cold sweat. Tears streamed down my face. Every time I shut my eyes, that image flashed before me. I stood up, I paced, I cried. I wanted to crawl out of my body. I wanted the vision to go away.

Finally, the sun came up. I felt physically better but my heart still ached and my disturbing dream scene was not fading. It was a Sunday morning. *I need to walk*, I said to myself. I thought I just needed to walk to a church. Any church. Any church that I arrived at first. It did not matter what time it was. It did not matter at what point the church would be at during the service. I did not care if there even was a service. I just knew I needed to be in the house of God. I needed God's help in processing my heartbreak.

"Please, God, be with me," I prayed. I was wandering the sidewalks of New York. It was a gray day, perfectly matching my mood. The air had a bite of cold, and the streets were quiet, as is often the case on an early New York City Sunday morning.

I stumbled into the first church I came upon. I made my way to a pew and quietly sat. It seemed it was the point in the service where the minister was about to deliver his message. The first line of his sermon went something like this; "I want to tell you about a movie I happened to see last night, called *Places in the Heart*."

I sat, stunned out of my sadness. The two of us had somehow, someway watched that old movie at the very same time. My heart pounded loudly. I struggled not to burst into tears.

He went on to describe the last scene in the film, a scene I was all too familiar with. I started breathing heavily and deeply, trying desperately not to faint. Right then and there the minster told us, told me, that at the end of the movie, when the dead were brought back to life, the movie was making a spiritual point. He went on to tell us that he felt it was an unforgettable statement of hope.

Unforgettable, all right! The scene was haunting me. My palms were sweaty. I was sweaty. I could not get right in my skin.

How was this happening? I wanted to jump up and say, "Is everyone seeing this? Is everyone hearing this?"

The minster continued, "This scene depicts the promise of Christianity. The promise that through God's grace, through Jesus, we are forgiven. *We are forgiven*," he repeated.

I could not hold any of it in anymore. My tears came rolling down. The image I had been given—of me seated on that church pew—was the "Blessed Assurance" that I was forgiven. I stumbled through taking communion while the hymn "Blessed Assurance" was sung.

That's right . . . the hymn "Blessed Assurance" was sung by the choir right then and there!

The lines from that hymn meant everything to me that day; the lines that promise: "Angels descending, bring from above echoes of mercy, whispers of love."

I was bathed in forgiveness which gave me the ability to move forward.

For Further Reflection

When have you felt you needed forgiveness?
How was God present in the delivery of your forgiveness?
How was His delivery a gift?

Put It into Practice

Look to God for forgiveness. Be alert for when and how God guides you toward the understanding and reassurance that forgiveness is yours when you seek it.

a loaf of bread

For as in Adam all die, so also in Christ shall all be made alive.

1 CORINTHIANS 15:22 ESV

When my aunt Ruth passed away, it felt like my own mother had left me. I had so much more I wanted to say to her. So much more I wanted to thank her for. I had so many unfinished conversations with her running through my mind. I think that is why I took her death so hard. Why had I not taken the time to express to her how she had shaped and soothed me throughout my life?

Everybody needs an Aunt Ruth. She was down to earth, but you always knew when she entered a room. She was not fancy, but had the grace of royalty. She was smart as a whip, but she did not wear it on her sleeve. She was a beauty, but did not lead with it. She had such dignity, but her humor could disarm you. She was my aunt as well as my Sunday school teacher, and I loved her. Her smile, her laugh, her touch, her understanding made me feel whole. We were lucky enough to live right next door to her for a spell. Man oh man, those were days I will never forget. My cousin Kassie, her daughter, recently told me that they had lived beside us for only a few years. Those years left such an impression on me that it felt like more. There was so much wisdom and many treasures that I learned from knowing her. I was not ready for her to be gone. I had not seen her much in my grown-up life, but I have had many conversations with her in my head. I have had many moments in which her character has informed my day.

There's one simple recipe that she passed on to my family that is emblematic of Aunt Ruth. It's a quick and easy recipe that reminds me of her in the best way possible: cinnamon quick bread.

Aunt Ruth's bread inspired many moments. One such moment occurred at my sister Marlee's rehearsal dinner, when her best friend Amy stood to give a toast. Amy told of the time when she first met Marlee. Amy and her family had just moved to our small town, when their doorbell rang. Amy sheepishly opened the door to find my sister standing there holding out a still-warm, just-out-of-the-oven loaf of Aunt Ruth's cinnamon bread.

In our neighborhood, when someone moved in, my mother would promptly bake Aunt Ruth's bread as a "welcome to the hood" gift. Bread was the perfect housewarming gift because it was as soothing and inviting as my aunt. Many friendships were initiated by these bread deliveries. But few were as enduring or as special as the forty-plus-year friendship of Marlee and Amy.

You see, my aunt Ruth was not at that rehearsal dinner, but her love was.

Another, rather symbolic way that my aunt Ruth's recipe helped is in the defining of my Katie Brown Brand.

When I first launched my business, I did it as an antidote to Martha Stewart's complicated and time-consuming perfectionist brand of domesticity. For my pilot episode of *Next Door with Katie Brown* on Lifetime Television, I needed to find a recipe that was simple and easy. The recipe also needed to be a bit snazzy and completely delicious. What should it be? Then it came to me: *Aunt Ruth's bread! Perfect!* The bread was full of flavor, but consisted of the humblest of ingredients. And the bread was a simple quick bread, which meant there was no need to knead it or wait for it to rise.

My aunt Ruth's down-to-earth character and practical manner were mirrored in that bread.

These characteristics made it the perfect recipe for me to include in the pilot episode of *Next Door with Katie Brown*, which turned into my first-ever TV series, which aired on Lifetime TV.

That cinnamon bread recipe from Aunt Ruth represented everything I wanted my brand of domesticity to be. My aunt Ruth was not there to bake the bread with me, but her brand of humility was.

To this day, her cinnamon bread is the most downloaded recipe on my website.

There is yet another less obvious, subtly abstract blessing I think of when I contemplate my aunt Ruth and her bread. The lesson, although it might seem absurd to some, is in the preparation of the bread.

To make the bread, you layer it. First a layer of the dough. Then a sprinkling of the cinnamon sugar mixture. Then a layer of dough. Then a sprinkling of the cinnamon sugar mixture. Again a layer of dough, then another sprinkling. Then you use a knife not to mix, but rather to kind of swirl the cinnamon sugar through the dough. When you slice the baked bread, you can see the golden-toned savory dough portion bleeding into the rich brown cinnamon sweet portion.

This technique mirrors the delicate balance that I strive for in so many areas of my life.

As a mother, when to nurture and when to show might.

As a boss, when to be quiet and follow and when to loudly lead.

As a friend, when to listen and when to help. Each time I prep the bread and get to the layering and swirling stages, I chuckle a bit to myself. I think, *I hear you, Ruth. I am trying to blend it well.*

My aunt Ruth is not with me when I struggle to find my life's perfect blend. But the lesson I've found in the swirling and baking of the equal parts savory and sweet of her bread stays with me.

I realize God does not always leave bread crumbs when you miss a loved one to help you find your way toward filling the gaps of loss. However, I am confident that God does give us glimpses in some form of the never-ending and ever-present love of meaningful people who have walked on.

A few nights after I returned home from Aunt Ruth's funeral, I put my three-year-old daughter Prentiss to bed. As I was tucking her in, she said that the night before she saw Aunt Ruth in her dreams. She told me how Aunt Ruth rode over to her on a very tall horse. Prentiss explained that my aunt hopped off her horse and gave my Prentiss the reins.

My aunt Ruth's love does not die. It lives on in heaven and is still felt here on earth.

For Further Reflection

Who in your life has physically passed on, but whose love is
   still with you?

How has God delivered the love to you from the person who
   has passed on?

How have the reminders of this person's character and being
   been a gift?

Put It into Practice

Honor the memory of those you love by recognizing their presence in your everyday life. Honor their memory by knowing
God allows their love to flow every day to you in so many
ways.

oranges and cucumbers

Finally, all of you should be of one mind. Sympathize with each other. Love each other as brothers and sisters. Be tenderhearted, and keep a humble attitude.

PETER 1 3:8 NLT

My husband; my two daughters, Prentiss, age ten, and Meredith, age five; and I recently relocated from Connecticut to Los Angeles for my work. When our first Sunday rolled around, the girls and I decided to give the AME church in downtown LA a try.

AME is short for African Methodist Episcopal, which is quite a combination of words. If you go to their website, you learn that the basis of this combo is that African means the church was organized by people of African descent, Methodist is included because the roots of the church are from the Methodist denomination, and Episcopal refers to the form of government that is the pattern for the AME denomination.

As the mother of an African-American daughter who was raised in a town on the East Coast with very few people of color, I thought I should now take advantage of being on the West Coast in a city that had a church made up of a majority of people who looked like my daughter.

I was grateful to land in a big city that was full of people from every part of the world who did not all look alike. I knew, as only a mother could, that my Meredith was being shaped by being the *different* one, by being the one who did not look like everyone else. Once, as I was giving Meredith a bath, she said to me, "When I grow up, my skin is going to be white." It was a devastating moment. I could not help but think that I had not done a good job at making her feel confident and proud of her brown skin. I was sure that her desire to have white skin was in part due to living in such a homogeneous part of the world.

So, off we three girls went to church, a church that I thought would be a very good experience for our little Meredith. When we rolled up to the AME, the parking lot was jam-packed full and then some. It seemed like there was a sea of African-American men, women, and children making their way to the entrance, all dressed to the nines. We parked as close as we could just a few blocks away, and joined the parade of people who were headed toward the AME front door.

My girls and I walked without talking. We were far too busy taking in all the beautiful women who wore hats and gloves and carried fancy handbags that matched their glorious shoes. They looked nothing like the reserved Waspy styles we saw in our Eastern home churches. It was a stream of vitality and bright colors that was moving all in the same direction. It was a breathtaking, powerful image we found ourselves floating in.

We entered through the center set of double doors and settled into a pew halfway between the doors and the altar. People were socializing from their pews. They were waving and chatting and greeting each other with so much love. The atmosphere was festive and the room was packed. It seemed like no sooner had everyone settled in than I heard the loveliest sound entering the church.

I turned around toward the sound to see a sea of black men and women working their way down the center aisle dressed in choir robes, clapping and singing *the most*, bestest gospel music you ever heard. Everyone in the church was rocking out. The entire congregation was standing, clapping, and swaying. The jubilance was awe-inspiring. There were two big screens at the front of the church that accentuated everything that was going on with the choir and preacher.

As the service began and the music continued to blow me away, I realized it was the Sunday just days after Martin Luther King Jr. Day. On the BIG screen we were treated to a montage of photos of him and the protests and his death. The reverence and tributes to him were moving and seemed to charge the mood in the sanctuary. As I looked around at the crowd, I suddenly realized Prentiss, my older daughter, and I were two of the very, very few white people in attendance.

The music continued to pulse in the most magnificent ways. The whole service was interactive, with people standing, raising their hands, shouting *"Alleluia!"* and the like when the Spirit moved them. They all seemed to be having such a spontaneous, natural, emotional reaction. At one point, Meredith turned to me, looked up, and said, "Can we come to this party every day?" I could see she was really soaking it all up. I thought to myself and the Lord, *Success!*

The service continued and the ministers drew parallels between the Civil Rights Movement of the sixties with the white man's racism of today that had manifested itself in the deadly police violence against, as they said, "Their children." It was tough to hear. I must admit, as one of the few white people in the room, I felt shame. My discomfort was soothed by the kind glances and the welcoming tones of the music. I mean, that music! It was perhaps one of the best concerts I had ever heard.

Next, they introduced a female athlete from the front podium. Through the introduction we learned she was the daughter of a civil rights activist and one of the first African-American women to win an Olympic medal. Again, everything was so inspiring and a bit overwhelming. Despite the tough subject of racism and the death of Martin Luther King Jr., the service was abundantly joyous. I felt grateful my daughters and I were able to witness it.

That night, when I put Meredith to bed, she told me how exciting she'd found the whole service. Later, I went in to tuck my fifth-grader Prentiss into bed. "Mom," she said, her bottom lip quivering, "I felt a little scared today at church." A tear ran down her cheek. She continued, "I felt like an orange in a cucumber crop. I felt judged. Do you think since we have white skin they will think we are responsible for all the horrible things that have happened to them? I really wanted to stand up and say, not us, it was not us."

I took a bit, gathered my thoughts. Then, I took a deep breath and slowly said, "Prentiss, imagine that that is how Meredith does feel and will feel most of the time."

"Exactly, Mom," she stated. "That is exactly what I thought. Meredith is always the orange."

My dear, perceptive Prentiss cried a bit as we held each other tight.

I thought I was being such a clever mother taking Meredith to a church full of cucumbers just like her. But, God knew, God knows that it was Prentiss, her big sister, who needed to experience being an orange. It was my Prentiss who needed to experience the sting of racism that her sister, Meredith, has and will experience far too often in her life. It was my Prentiss who needed to experience this harsh truth in the loving comfort of God's home in order to truly gain insight into her sister Meredith's life.

For Further Reflection

When did you recognize the struggle of another?
How was God in this recognition?
How is this new knowledge a gift?

Put It into Practice

Walk in someone else's shoes so that God can expose you to the vantage point of others. He will enlighten you through that view, which will enrich your life in a deep and consequential way.

DEFEAT

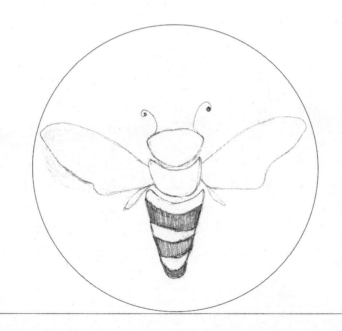

a beehive

In the same way, faith by itself, if it is not accompanied by action, is dead.

JAMES 2:17 NIV

By the time I was in fifth grade, church had become my happy place. I loved it. I was not a star at regular school. Each subject discussed just kind of flew right over my head. But at church, in Sunday school, I was the BOMB. I could barely speak at my regular school. I felt self-conscious, lost, lonely, and bored. However, at Sunday school, I knew what time it was. I could follow the thinking. I was on the edge of my seat waiting to see what revelations the next verse and chapter would spark. I felt passion for the subject. I could not wait to engage in the deep discussion that would inevitably occur.

The story of John the Baptist blew my young mind. Moses and his staff turned on my imagination. The parting of the Red Sea was epic! I soaked up the characters, the landscape, and the events that unfolded in the Bible stories I was learning. I often felt like I was part of these tales, as they were being taught to me. I asked questions, interjected comments, and led discussions Sunday after Sunday. My opinion, my voice, mattered in the walls of my church classrooms.

I felt like my school teachers barely knew my name. But my

Sunday school teachers? Their eyes would light up when I spoke. If only the calendar were reversed and school was one day a week and Sunday school was five days a week, I would be golden. That kind of a rework would be my fifth grade heart's idea of heaven.

For as long as I can remember, I felt most at home when I was thinking and talking about GOD. I felt a kind of caring vibe when I entered our creaky old church on Mitchell Street. It was almost as if the panic that I carried with me most of my days kind of turned off as I would tune into the hum and rhythm of the white walls and purple-covered pews that lined our church sanctuary.

Until one sunny spring day when all that changed.

On this seemingly typical Sunday, my teacher, who I always remember as being named Mrs. Singer because she owned the Singer sewing shop on Mitchell Street, was a petite, soft-spoken woman with a subtle smile. This particular spring Sunday she had scheduled a special guest to appear in our classroom. The guest, it turned out, was a beekeeper. The keeper stood in front of us as we sat crisscross applesauce, listening to him teach us everything about the life of bees.

He spent a good deal of the hour talking about the relationship between the queen bee and the worker bees. He explained how the queen bee was like God and the worker bees were like us. He said that, like the worker bee, who spends all of its time out collecting pollen to bring home to the queen bee, a good Christian should spend all of their time out talking, thinking, and convincing others to come home to Jesus. He claimed this kind of devotion was the only way for a Christian to enjoy life's honey. He reiterated his analogy by stating that, just like the worker bee who is singular in its mission to gather the pollen, a good Christian had to be singular in knowing that the only thing that truly matters was their work for God. The beekeeper taught us that, just like the bee, we must devote our entire being, aspirations, and daily existence to God's work.

WHAT! HUH! The earth shook. I loved God and the church and everything about it. It was such an important part of my world. But to be honest, I was also a ski racer, a painter, a cook. So to me, the operative word in that sentence is "part." Really, *everything*? Was he serious? Everything I did and every day I lived was to be all about God?

Maybe I had to rethink my center. I was only in fifth grade. But still, I did have a few thoughts about what and how I wanted to live my life. Now Mr. Beekeeper was telling us that none of my dreams or ideas mattered.

I ran out of the church and up the street to my house in tears. It seemed I was not a rock-star Sunday school student after all, because I hated what I'd just heard.

My mother met me at the door. "I am out!" I told her. "This is crazy. NO. Nope. NO. I will not be a part of something that seems so selfish and one-sided and demanding. What about me?" I pleaded. "I mean, it is a big world out there and I might have some plans of my own."

Somehow, my mother calmed me down long enough to explain that God would work with me, and my true desires are God's true desires for me. *Blah. Blah. Blah.*

Yet I did go back to my church on Mitchell Street. I simply put one foot in front of the other, and the knot in my stomach soon loosened and the pit in my stomach soon faded. As I continued to sing in the choir, plate cookies during coffee hour, and help out in the nursery, I held on to the truth that church was my happy place despite not fully understanding what I had just learned from the beekeeper. Slowly, my Christian spiritual balance returned.

That day the beekeeper guest speaker scared me badly, and I wanted to run away as fast as I could. I have often looked back on that experience, not to try to understand the relationship between bees and Christianity, but to embrace the truth that would finally move me forward and set me free: When I am participating and at the front of the class of a faithful life, I need to be ready for my commitment, and the intensity of that commitment, to hit back and challenge me.

I learned that day that my faith would be tested. However, if I could hold on to my faith's pure instincts, that told me to return to the rituals that my devotion desired without having all the answers, then in time, my peace would be restored.

The mere act of going through the motions delivered me back to my center. In the end, I was like the worker bee flying back to my queen without fully understanding why.

For Further Reflection

When has your faith required you to be or do something you did not fully understand?

How did God shed light on your understanding?

How was this new awareness a gift?

Put It into Practice

Look to your faith instead of looking for answers to settle your fears. Hold on to the habits and rituals that your beliefs have taught you when answers seem elusive. Patiently exercise the everyday practices in order to obtain a deeper understanding.

a mountaintop

Two are better than one, because they have a good return for their labor: If either of them falls down, one can help the other up. But pity anyone who falls and has no one to help them up.

ECCLESIASTES 4:9–10 NIV

When I was in high school, I was at my core a bit of a loner. I was most content when I was by myself, happiest alone in my room. Walking solo to school was always my first choice. This was a bit confusing to me and most of the people who knew me, because I was that kid who appeared to be quite popular. Strangely, though, I felt sometimes homesick even when I was at home. I felt OUT even when I was IN.

My first sleepover was at the home of a girl named Beth. From the minute I walked in, I knew I had made a mistake. I got through the night, not because I wanted to, but because my parents would not come get me.

My first sleep-away-from-home camp was a disaster, too. I hated every minute of it. The kids, the closeness, the togetherness... there was just no escaping it all. It was my worst.

Throughout most of high school, I attended a West Coast ski camp. This, I know, sounds really glamorous. And in some ways it was. But the truth is that we were fed peanut butter and pickle sandwiches. *WHAT?* And we slept with what seemed like thirty girls in a room that had bunks four high with only one bathroom.

We were up at 5 a.m. and rode in buses that wound and twisted their way up steep mountain roads to get us to the base, where we'd catch the chair lifts. The entire drive I had to hold my head out the window because most mornings I became so car sick, and that was the only way I could get relief.

I could hang on at ski camp a bit better because both my sisters were with me. Plus, I wanted to become a great ski racer, so I would mentally "muscle through" being surrounded by my peers twenty-four/seven, because I knew that the constant practice and coaching could help me accomplish my goal.

And while we are on the subject of my love of ski racing, it should be noted that it is an *individual* sport. That's right, you probably already guessed it—any team sport I tried just drove me crazy. I wanted to be *the* best. I and I alone finished first in ski races. I liked that. I did not want to learn to be part of the whole. I am sure an insightful person might have guessed I was...

Too scared to be too close.

Too self-conscious to really feel I could be part of a crowd.

Too frightened by the thought that if people knew me well, they might see who I really was and choose not to include me.

So, I learned how to keep my distance.

On this particular glamorous summer morning as the sun came up, we were catching the first chair-lift ride up the glacier and carrying salt bags that weighed more than us (our coaches would apply the salt throughout the day to keep the snow from melting on the courses they set). I could see that already twelve or so ski-racing lanes were buzzing with activity. Two of the lanes were ours, and had been set up by our coach as slalom runs. Another one of the twelve lanes was occupied by some really fast female racers from the Green Mountain Ski School on the East Coast. Another few lanes were occupied by none other than the US Ski Team.

As the morning unfolded, I was really struggling. My beloved but extremely tough Austrian ski coach told me I was embarrassing him in front of those superior teams. On another run, his critique was that I looked like a sack of potatoes rolling down the hill. Yes, "like a sack of potatoes!" UGH. This was not my day.

When I arrived at the top of the course, for what was sure to be another disastrous run, it appeared that a new set of courses had been set by my coach. He radioed up that he wanted me to get in the starting gate at the same time as a girl named Heidi. Unbeknownst to me, he had set up a dual slalom for us. For those of you who do not know what that is, allow me to explain: It is when two identical race courses are set up right next to each other so that competitors can enter at the same time and can see, in real time, who is winning.

I must tell you that Heidi was the very best ski racer training with us that day. She was on the US Ski Team and wore the uniform to prove it. She was light-years faster than I was. Why oh why did he want me to race her down this mountain? More humiliation was most definitely in my future! *OH NO, no, no please do not make me,* I thought. I felt ill as I slid into the gate. I knew I was about to be crushed.

"Three-two-one-GO!"

We pushed out of the starting gate at the same time. *Oh dear God, please allow me to hold on to a bit of my dignity here!* I took my first turn at about the same time I felt her take the first turn. Then the next.

I edged. I grunted. I carved. I was getting into a rhythm.

I turned left. She turned left. Right. Right. Left. Left. I was keeping up! She was right there at my side!

Faster! Hold it. Punch it!

She and I pushing in what felt like tandem timing. We both skied through the finish gate at the same time.

Holy smokes!

My coach skied up, looked me straight in the eye, and motioned for me to get back up to the top. "Now do you see? I want you to do that again and again and again!" he said.

I could barely breathe. I was in a bit of a trance as I made my way to the bottom of the chair lift. In that dual race I realized that by pairing this loner *me* with someone better than *me*, my coach had raised my game and showed me how high I could really go.

Who knew?

It seems I needed to do the dance with someone else leading in order for me to reach the pace I needed to make my solo journey to first place. I needed a peer, a friend, a fellow racer to push me up to it!

I have learned through the years that God is much like my Austrian ski coach, because God also pairs me at the perfect time with a perfect teammate or mates, to get me to where I need to go.

So, no matter how overwhelming it might seem to get in the starting gate of a relationship that will push you forward, go for it! Do it with all you've got. Push as hard as you can to stay close, to keep up, to show up, and see the friendship through—because you never know what new speed your life might take.

Do not get me wrong. I am still a loner at heart, and I do not think that will ever change. But ever since that day, I try to push and challenge myself to overcome my social fear so that I may be made better by those around me.

It is when we ski down the mountain while being pushed and challenged by others that we get to be the best of the best, which is what God wants for us.

For Further Reflection

Which relationships in your life have taken you higher and made you sharper?

How has God coached you to get closer to those people in your life who raise your game?

How has this pairing with others lifted you to new heights and been a gift to the way you live your life?

Put It into Practice

Seek out people who possess qualities that you admire. Then mimic their talents and grace so that you can rise further toward the potential God knows you are capable of.

an apple tree

But if some of the branches were broken off, and you, being a wild
olive, were grafted in among them and became partaker with them of
the rich root of the olive tree, do not be arrogant toward the branches;
but if you are arrogant, remember that it is not you who supports the
root, but the root supports you. You will say then, "Branches were
broken off so that I might be grafted in."

ROMANS 11:17–19 NASB

I struggled to get pregnant after the birth of my daughter Prentiss. Prentiss was born on Mother's Day, in the same year I turned forty. My husband and I knew that if we wanted more children, we had to start trying very soon after her birth because of my age. But it was not easy.

I suffered three devastating miscarriages. Then I became pregnant with twins. I was thrilled because my grandfather had been a twin. Moreover, two of my favorite people were red-headed twins and they had such a strong bond. I thought how lucky my babies would be to have each other to travel through life with. Soon, it, too, ended in first one and then another miscarriage.

The heartache was almost unbearable. Those were dark, dark days that seemed heavy with melancholy and gloom. Those were days where I was full of a deep sadness at the loss I'd been forced to accept over and over again.

I felt buried in self-pity and could not seem to rise up from my hopeless state. My husband was eager to give adoption a try, but I was slow to warm to the idea. I was still walking through the pain of our failed pregnancies. Somehow, he was all systems go.

So, I followed. Reluctantly.

We went through the initial meetings. We plowed through the towers of paperwork, and nervously smiled while answering numerous mind-numbing questions concerning our motivations for taking on the challenges of parenting an adopted child. We were on the ready, but my heart was still not really in it.

You see. I come from a BIG Midwestern family. We all look vaguely the same. I've always found comfort in that sameness, comfort in knowing where my roots began, who my clan was. How would it be raising a child who had none of that familiarity?

I know.

I know.

What I was thinking was not very evolved.

The best part of me was ready to jump in, to love any baby who needed us. At the same time, my heart ached to carry our next child in my belly, to give birth to my baby, to breastfeed my baby, to know my baby in a deep DNA way. That is the way I knew things to be. That is the way I knew how it should look. That is the way I knew how to do it. And yet we pushed forward.

While we were staying at a small apple orchard we had just purchased in Western Massachusetts, we spoke to a potential birth mother. The phone call went well. It seemed there was at least the potential for a match. It was not our first brush with the possibility of finding our baby. We had traveled down the adoption road with more than one set of birth parents, which had only led to more heartache. This woman, this call, this time around felt, dare I say, it felt terrifyingly possible. My heart leapt at the idea that we could soon hold a baby in our arms, while my head swirled with concerns about how it would all work.

We hung up the phone with this woman just minutes before we were to walk through the orchard with the previous owners, Lou and Sue Chadwick. We were going to learn more about the rows of trees that were now under our care. The doorbell rang. There stood Lou and Sue, the apple orchard owners. I was in a bit of a daze as we walked out into the day and into the rows and rows of their homegrown apple trees. The sun was shining, but I cannot tell you if it was warm or cold. I managed to walk and exchange pleasantries despite my conflicted heart. I could not help but want to shout, *I will care for your trees! I will treat them like they are mine. I will nurture them like I have known them from the day they were planted in the ground. I will be the best caregiver to your trees that you could have ever hoped for!*

The Chadwicks had started the apple orchard on a piece of land they inherited from Sue's father. It was an heirloom apple orchard. I had no idea what that meant when we bought it.

As Lou and Sue walked us up and down the rows of trees, they explained to us that this valley in Massachusetts used to be the home of many storied apple orchards. Over the years, several of those orchards had gone out of business. With those closures, many varieties of apples would disappear. So they made it their business to graft various apple types together onto one tree. Hence, the creation of their heirloom apple orchard.

We stood in front of a grand apple tree with not one, not two, but *four* different types of apples growing on one tree! Lou and Sue went into more detail, describing the grafting technique. They told how a section of a stem or leaf buds is inserted into the stock of a tree. The upper part of the graft becomes the top of the plant; the lower portion becomes part of the root system. They boasted that by grafting these foreign branches onto an existing tree or, as they say in the business, the "root tree," they had created not only a more interesting and enjoyable tree but a stronger tree.

"When these mix-matched branches combine into one, they strengthen the trunk and the root system. Trees that are not grafted will not produce fruit for about ten years. A grafted apple tree? It will begin to bear fruit after four years," Lou said.

My heart swelled. My eyes filled with tears. I felt a little light-headed. Sue and Lou were describing my growing family!

This bold tree that stood in front of me with all its diverse, divinely inspired limbs was teaching me by illustrating to me quite literally how welcoming apple strains that need a new home, a new base to grow from . . . strengthen my familial roots.

My intrepid soul found peace in this shining tree's example.

These two salty Yankees had no idea that what they were passing on to me that day was so much more than the art of grafting.

I could not wait to get back to that phone, to let our adoption team know I was all systems GO!

We brought our daughter Meredith home less than a year later, who, just like the grafted heirloom apple trees in our orchard, was fruit given much sooner than we had expected.

For Further Reflection

When did you fear something would not fit?
How does God fit into your experience?
How is this new journey a gift?

Put It into Practice

Embrace your fear of the different to find the strength to move forward into what God is orchestrating for you. God will not leave you for a minute.

a basement

Thus says the Lord God: The gate of the inner court that faces east shall be shut on the six working days, but on the Sabbath day it shall be opened, and on the day of the new moon it shall be opened.

EZEKIEL 46:1 ESV

It was a breezy, cold fall Saturday, and I had flown to Ann Arbor to surprise my mom and dad, who were attending a University of Michigan football game. I arrived at the stadium and sat down right next to them. It was fun to see their shocked and thrilled faces. However, it was more than just a casual visit to see a game and my parents. It was a visit to come check in on my mom. She had been diagnosed with cancer and had just had a radical hysterectomy at the University of Michigan Hospital, which was about five hours away from the small island in Michigan where they lived. When I saw her that day, it took my breath away, not because I was filled with joy, but because I was filled with fear. She looked so thin, so frail.

My fragile mom was staying with my younger sister, who lived one town over from the University Hospital, which made hospital visits easier. After the game, my dad returned to the island for work, while my mom slept in my sister's basement.

The next morning after the game, I left my hotel room early to pick my mom up from my sister's to take her to church.

I remember it was dark, and there was a brisk chill in the air. I found my mom still asleep. I gently woke her; it was all I could do not to scoop her up right there, right then, and cradle her. She woke up, stood, and forced herself to get dressed. It was excruciating to watch. I felt so helpless, so frustrated, so at a loss. Everything felt wrong. My mighty mother seemed beat, seemed meek, seemed gone.

She and my father had been engaged in a four- to five-year struggle. Not concerning health; that challenge was new. Their years-long debate was about how and where to live now that they were empty nesters. My father still needed to work, but I think he wanted and needed a change. So he left his law practice to run a boat line, which took passengers and freight to an island in Michigan. His new job meant that my parents had to relocate to the island, where only bikes and horses and buggies were allowed. The island booms with life in the summer and is desolate in the winter. Dad liked life there. My mom liked it, too, but she missed her busy year-round life.

They had many a heated discussion about when, how, and where else they could live so that my dad could continue to work but Mom could be on the mainland and have more robust days. Do not get me wrong. Mom loved the island for its beauty, community, and history, but the dark and long winters could get her down at times. Dad dug his heels in. They were staying put all year round, he insisted.

It was odd to watch my parents having trouble helping themselves, to witness them having arguments, making life choices that were not propelling them forward. They were stuck. And now this. Now this illness. They needed relief, but clearly they were not moving toward seeking it.

These were my parents. They were my king and queen. Yet now these larger-than-life parents of mine seemed small, lost, needy. There in that dark basement it hit me: it was now my turn, my place, my role, to step in and do what they could not.

I did not lament it. I did not converse with anyone. It was instinctual, primal, maybe even impulsive.

"Mom," I said, "we are going to a different kind of church today. We are going to go to a church called 'The first day of the rest of your life.' God's going to be with us, as we go and search and plot. Mom, today I am buying you a house. I am getting you off that island. I am finding you a place to rest close to your doctors."

"Oh, Katie, don't be silly," she said. "You are not buying me a house."

"Yes I am today, in Ann Arbor, which is the home of both your and Dad's alma mater. The home of a giant award-winning hospital. Dad loves it there. You love it there."

"Katie," Mom whispered, "NO. You are crazy. We are living on the island."

"Fine," I replied. "Continue to live on the island. But when you are not, when you are down here, in treatment, you will stay in your house that I am going to buy for you today."

She then said, "You cannot afford that, Katie."

Ah, a crack. She's thinking about it, I thought.

"See, Mom," I said, "that's where you're wrong." You see, I was about six months into the filming of my hit TV show on Lifetime called *Next Door with Katie Brown*, and I was making enough money to make it happen. "YES, MOM!" I said defiantly, "I can afford it. I am single. I know nothing about the stock market. But I do know something about houses. So, I know it will be a great investment."

"NO, NO, NO, NO, Katie," she said as she shook her head. "I cannot let you do that."

"You do not have a choice. I am buying you a house today."

"Your father does not want to live there. He wants to live on the island," Mom argued.

"So let him. But you...you need to be by your doctors. You need to be in the thick of it. You need to be active in a church you love, and Ann Arbor has all that. So, YES, I am buying you a house."

"Oh, Katie," she sighed.

There it was again. I felt a bit of an opening. So I quickly followed up with, "Today, we are finding a house. If you want to live in it, great! If not, I will look at it as a great investment, in a groovy college town."

Sure, I was sounding really confident, but I had *no* idea what I was saying. It was true I could afford it, or at least I thought I could. I mean, I was planning on buying a house in Los Angeles for me. Surely a house in Michigan had to be less than that? I decided I would just put off buying my digs and get my mom and, I believed, eventually my dad settled.

But it was a Sunday. Most of the area was asleep and taking the day off. Plus, I did not know anyone in or anything about Ann Arbor. Furthermore, I had to be back in front of a camera to continue shooting my show on Monday morning, so I had to fly out that night. No later. Lynnie and Marlee, my two sisters, had gone to the University of Michigan. They had spent several years in Ann Arbor, so they might know someone.

Nope. Marlee knew no one.

Next up, Lynnie. Luckily it turned out that she and her husband, who were living in New York City, had looked into moving back to Ann Arbor a few times, so she did have the number of the Realtor who had shown them around. Lynnie said, "I haven't talked to her in years, but I still have her number."

Ring, ring. "Hello." I got her. "Hi, I am Lynn Brown's sister."

"Yep, I remember her," she replied.

"I gotta buy my mom a house TODAY!" I stated.

"Today?" She laughed.

"Seriously," I said, "TODAY."

"Sundays are busy," was her response.

"I'll buy you lunch," I pleaded.

"What type of house?" she asked.

"A cheap one, a fixer-upper (that is what I do, after all). A traditional one with a central hall. My mom loves a central hall," I explained.

I was daydreaming that it could look and feel like the house Mom raised us in, because she missed it so much.

"Hmmm," she said.

"I'll buy you a house today, too, if you help me out," I joked while holding my breath in hopes she would say yes. "Oh, and it needs to be very near the University Hospital. Preferably within walking distance." I held my breath longer while saying a little prayer.

"Hmmm," she said. It was clear she was thinking. "Okay, let me see what I can do. But it will be hard to set up appointments because most agents are holding open houses on Sunday or with clients with previously scheduled appointments."

I began to pray harder. "God? This feels right. I believe I am following the Holy Spirit, who is with me in this cold basement, leading me toward some kind of transformation for both my mom and me. My mom needs my help. Help me help her. Today is a Sunday, Your day. We will walk in whatever direction as far as You need us to. We will walk toward the light. Please show us the path."

Within the hour, we were in the car riding toward the first house. My mom shook her head and mumbled to herself the whole way about how dumb this idea was.

The first two houses, not so much. The next one, closer, but too expensive. "Katie, this is just not possible," Mom grumbled.

I prayed and said, "Is this a no-go, God?"

The fourth house? The fourth house was on a dead-end street, and Mom liked that. I was a bit turned around, as I really did not know the town, but it seemed to me it was four or five blocks from the hospital. Right when we pulled up, I thought it was so charming that I found it hard to believe I could afford it. I walked through the front door. Much to my delight, it had a central hall, a living room to one side, and a dining room to the other. The exact layout of the home I grew up in, but scaled down. It was old and full of creaks and cracks. But it had great bones and beautiful vintage windows. It was a little house with everything I had day-dreamed about. It was perfect.

It turned out that no one had lived in it for two years. *For two years*, I thought. *What are the chances that a house this close to campus would be sitting on the market for that long?* For two years, the house had waited patiently for us. For two years, this house prepared for our arrival.

SOLD! SOLD! To us! Thank You, God!

My mom's eyes opened wide and wild. "Katie," she scolded, "I have gone along this long, but NO!"

I paid no mind to her talk or tone, and within the week the house was all ours.

Now, my dad was not happy that I had jumped right smack dab into the center of their marital spat. But like I said, that Sunday's lesson at the church of the first day of the rest of our life was this: It was my turn. My mom and dad needed me. God and I knew best. I mean, what are the chances? Who finds a house, in a town they do not know, on a Sunday, that they can afford, that had the qualities they want, and that is located right smack dab where they need it to be?

In the beginning, only my mom lived there. But in time, my dad spent more time there than he did at his island home.

My mom? She got better. And my parents' marriage? It thrived in the garden of that college town with sporting events and intellectual lectures to pursue.

My day off, my mom's day off, God's day was our day. Our day for a new beginning. A new roof for Mom and Dad. And a new role for me from cared-for daughter to caregiving daughter. Within a few years, my parents purchased the house. A few years later, my father retired from that island to live full-time in that university town, in the house we found on the Sabbath with the Holy Spirit helping a real estate agent answer the phone, being our tour guide and opening the doors.

A few years later my parents added a first-floor master suite so they could grow old right there, next to the University Hospital, in the house with a central hall, and I in the central role of daughter turned usher.

For Further Reflection

When and how have you broken free from a difficult place? How has God helped you define your new role and direction? How has this shift been a gift?

Put It into Practice

Cultivate people, thinking, and habits that propel you forward. Call out and hang on to God's hand so that you can hear his direction—a direction that will lead you to the next stage of the rest of your life, no matter how impossible it may seem.

a talk

As each has received a gift, use it to serve one another, as good
stewards of God's varied grace.

PETER 4:10 ESV

In July, a few years back, I got a call from a woman representing
our community church. She asked me if I would be willing to
talk to their adult Bible study about my faith. "Why of course,"
was my response. With that, we confirmed a date in March.

In February, I got a call from that same woman asking me
for the title of my talk. Title? Title? Oh dear, I had forgotten all
about this talk…this commitment. *Oh why do I keep my calendar in*
such a jumbled and haphazard way? She explained they needed the
title promptly in order to send out an e-mail publicizing my talk,
which was only a month away.

"A title?" I asked, trying to bide my time in hopes something
would pop into my brain.

"Yes, a title," she replied.

"Was there something in particular you wanted me to talk
about?" I asked, stalling.

She answered, "We were thinking you could speak about food
and the Bible."

"Food and the Bible. Hmmm," I pondered. "I do not know anything about food and the Bible."

There was, as you might imagine, silence on the other end of the phone. I could sense her disappointment. Since I have a cooking show and I write cookbooks, I get what she was getting at. But me and food and the Bible? I got nothin'! After a bit of conversation, we settled on "God Is the Ultimate Lifestyle Expert." You see, the title was one I used almost ten years earlier, the first and only other time I had spoken about my faith publicly. My mother had asked me to be a breakout speaker at her "WinSome Women Retreat."

Six times in one weekend, I stood in front of some three hundred women to open up about my previously very private walk with God. I told five stories that I call *God Moments*, or moments I had experienced that highlighted my faith. All five stories had a profound impact on my life. *Yes!* I thought, *that is the talk I will revisit for the Congregational Church Adult Bible Study speech.*

The woman from the church seemed to accept this title with trepidation. Again, I felt her frustration that I was not embracing their concept of food in the Bible. But "God Is the Ultimate Lifestyle Expert" it would be.

In the week that followed, I had to return to my home state of Michigan, where I had been hired to give a speech on all things *Katie Brown Workshop*. My typical talking topics covered cooking, gardening, decorating, and some of the highlights of my career. Simple, really. I would, as always, bring along a few DIY projects to demonstrate that would accentuate my talking points.

That cold February morning in Michigan, I was dog tired. I just realized that they had contracted for me to talk a full hour. I also just realized that there would be thirteen hundred women in attendance, as opposed to my usual three hundred. So much for reading the fine print.

How is that going to work? I thought as we drove to the venue where I would be delivering my talk. If there were that many people, how would they see the little flower arrangements and crafts I was planning on creating, which really were the fuel that helped make my points and moved my talk along at these types of events? I could not believe there would really be thirteen hundred people there. I walked into the auditorium as all those people were filing in.

Wait. What? The woman running the event confirmed that all my props and crafts supplies would *never* work because no one would be able to see them.

She felt it would be best if I just talk. *Just* talk for a whole hour? In front of thirteen hundred women? *Remain calm. Okay,* I thought, *I know what I can do. I will print out the manuscript to a new book I'm working on and read from it.* With minutes to go, the stage manager, who I had asked to help me out by printing it, handed me the pages. *Oh dear,* I realized it was very dark up there at the podium. *Oh dear,* it appeared my script had been printed on both sides of the page. *Oh dear, oh dear,* I thought as I stumbled through the beginning words of my speech. Then I lost my place. Next, I forgot to flip some pages over. My logic was jumbled and I was dying up here. One hour of sheer pain for the audience and me followed. One hour for all thirteen hundred women to listen to me trip through my words and thoughts.

The humiliation set in before I had even left the stage. The memory continued to haunt me when I returned home. I had to take to my bed and remain in the fetal position until all the images of the stunned and silent faces in the crowd faded. I failed. I failed BADLY!

Please trust me when I say:

I know how to talk in front of a crowd.

I know how to entertain them.

I know how to move them.

I know when I have blown it.

I knew I let every person down in that room.

I awoke to an e-mail from the local community church lady:

"Do you need any AV equipment?" she asked. "Do you need a podium? Do you need any help?"

OH NO! I had to give another talk. I had forgotten, or maybe purposely put it out of my mind. *How can I get out of it? I cannot get up in front of people again.* I went back to sleep.

The talk was one week away. With the sting of my recent failure in my gut, I got busy. I was motivated. I needed to prove to myself that I could do it. That I could still hold an audience. That I could deliver a home-run speech. I was so driven, I recited the talk while standing in front of my mirror. I devoted so much thought and time to the writing of those stories. I worked on them nonstop.

My husband thought I was nuts. "Why?" he asked. "Why are you spending so much time on this little talk that so few people will attend?"

I could not stop long enough to explain it. So, I just ignored his ridiculing vibes and questions. I simply charged on. He will never understand how much it cut that I had failed so miserably in Michigan. I had to prove to myself that I had the ability to hold a crowd, no matter what the size. Plus, it was for God. I could not let my God down.

Faith to me has always been a private thing. Something deeply personal. Something seriously intimate. I have fiercely guarded my relationship with God. God and me. Me and God. Maybe, I have even been a bit selfish, haughty even with my feelings about

God. Like we had the most special of relationships. My conversations, my walk, my love affair with the Trinity have always been mine and mine alone.

Yes, I have always gone to church. I have been active in my church community. I have been a Sunday school teacher, a coffee hour leader, and a head chef for weekly church dinners. But to share with others the true depth of my faith, no siree Bob. Yes, I had tiptoed around it by opening up at one of those WinSome Women Retreats, but that was ten years earlier. I had to do this. I had to do this well, and for so many reasons.

The morning came, and it was freezing. To make matters worse, it was daylight saving Sunday, which meant adult Sunday school would really be at 8:30 a.m. but it would feel like 7:30 a.m. and due to the early hour there would be most likely ten folks at best as opposed to the normal twenty or so.

Much to my husband's dismay, I woke him. "I am not coming," he sputtered. "You do not need me to come."

"YES, YES I do," I said. "You know how much this means to me."

He rolled his eyes. He shook his head NO. But he got dressed and the whole way there . . . we argued.

I was SO mad at him.

"The girls should be coming, too. It is a good talk. I think they should hear it," I said emphatically.

"NO," he said.

We drove on in silence.

There were maybe fifteen people there. My husband played a short video reel that was a montage of my career highlights. The church lady gave me a lovely introduction. As she spoke, I realized I was so nervous that my hands were shaking. I did not want to let the Good Lord above down. *Please God, be with me*, I thought.

I told my first story while a Bible verse that summed it up flashed on the screen behind me. I read the next story and the next. My hands shook and my knees were weak. I so hoped no one noticed, but then I realized that was quite impossible since the papers I was holding moved with each one of my quivers.

I had most of my talk memorized. So, I had the freedom to look around and move about as I rolled through my presentation. The people laughed. They gasped. They seemed to be soaking it up. Two of my good friends and one of their daughters, who sat in the front row, seemed into it...

I got it. I got this. DONE! Phew. I think I nailed it!

The minute I finished, my friend in the front row flew up with both fists raised and shouted, "Vindicated!"

Alleluia...Amen! YES! YES! YES! Thank You, God.

It turns out I could do IT. I still had IT. God is good and God is great.

I strolled through a question-and-answer period. The feedback was fantastic. If I do say so myself, I had moved this crowd. I had not let the Good Lord Above down. As the people began to leave, many of them came up to thank me. To tell me of their own God Moments. To ever so graciously say, "Well done."

Then one woman came up and said, "Do you know my name?"

"NO," I said. (I mean, I knew she was the woman who had introduced me.) But I did not know or remember her name.

"I am the woman you have been coordinating with over e-mail concerning this morning's talk," she said. "I am Bridget Johnson."

"Of course. Yes," I said. "So sorry."

"Do you know what I do?" she asked.

"No," I said.

"Oh well, have you ever heard of a man named Rick Warren?"

"No," was again my answer.

My husband, who was standing next to me, nodded his head "yes."

"He wrote a book called *The Purpose Driven Life*. Have you heard of that?"

"No," I answered.

My husband spoke up, "Yes, of course," and with those words, he became very interested.

"Well," she continued, "I worked on projects with him. And I think your stories could come together in a book. I could maybe help you. Do you have more stories?"

"I have a lifetime of stories," was my answer.

"Well, how about you write about ten of them up and send them to me?" she said.

"Yes," my husband answered for me.

I spent about a week writing ten stories and sent them off to Ms. Johnson. She quickly responded. And the next thing I knew, the three of us, William, Ms. Johnson, and myself, were sitting down in our living room. She told us how she thought my stories were wonderful and that they should be shared. She really felt my stories would be meaningful to many. I was blown away...

So frightened.

So excited.

So humbled.

So emotional.

"Would you help?" I asked. "I do not think I would have the nerve to do this on my own."

"Yes, I could try. But I am not an agent," she cautioned. "I think you need an agent to get it sold."

"No," I said with surprising confidence. "I think I need you."

She agreed and promptly sent it out to five publishers. Our first meeting was with Hachette, and I could barely contain myself. During the meeting they told me how much they liked my book and wanted to buy it. Within days they made me an offer.

When I fell in front of those thirteen hundred people that day in Michigan, I fell far.

That fall awakened me.

That fall humbled me.

I leaned into God while failing and failing my fall and failure and God broke my fall, lifted me up and shifted my focus… guided me to a new path that resulted in a need and a task that has drawn me closer to myself.

And yes, kicked me into high gear.

And blew my mind, opened my heart, and enabled my soul to embrace a bigger, better, bolder labor of love that I could never, ever have imagined.

For Further Reflection

When have you bumped into or uncovered a talent of yours?
How did God help deliver, find, and develop that talent?
How has your God-given talent been a gift?

Put It into Practice

Be open to digging deeper into your skills in order to go higher
and walk closer with God, who wants you to own all you
possess.

a class

An intelligent heart acquires knowledge, and the ear of the wise seeks knowledge.

PROVERBS 18:15 ESV

It was the morning of my first class at Cornell University, and day one of my first bout of nerves. I wondered, would I be good enough for this amazing university I had landed in?

Perhaps my nerves were encouraged by the fact that when I first arrived, I attended a big orientation assembly in a cavernous hall for all incoming freshmen. The president of the university stood up at the podium and asked all the students who had graduated third in their class to raise their hands. Next, he requested that everyone who was second in their class to raise their hands. Now whoever was first to raise their hands. Then he said something to the effect of: "Take a look around. This student body is made up of some of the best of the best from all around the world, so bring it!"

It seemed everyone had raised their hand except me. *Gulp.* As I sat and stared at the sea of hands in the air, I thought, *I am in over my head.* He went on to say, "Bring the best you have, give it all you've got, and you will leave here armed with the ability to play with the best of them."

I think I started praying right then and there, *God, please do not let me fail. Please allow me to hang in, please walk with me as I maneu-ver my way through this splendid educational opportunity.*

Now here I was trying to find my way to my first class and I was hopelessly lost. The clock was ticking. Where oh where was I? *Where is the room where my freshman English class is?* I sweated. I paced.

I found it! Yeah!...but I was late. The door was closed. The class was clearly under way.

What to do? What to do? UGH. Okay. Okay. I will wait, and when class is over, I will introduce myself to the professor and apologize for being late. I realized that clearly none of my other stupendous fel-low freshmen had had a hard time finding their way. I settled in and sat on the floor next to the classroom door. My silent self-loathing was interrupted by a loud sound.

Clip clop.

Clip clop.

Clip clop.

The sound grew louder and louder. I looked up to see someone walking toward me.

Clip clop.

Clip clop.

The footsteps stopped right in front of me. I looked up to see a fellow coed starring down at me. "What are you doing down there?" she asked.

"Well, you see," I explained, "I am late and I did not want to disturb the teacher or the class. It seemed best to just sit out here and wait until the class is over, and then I will introduce myself. It felt like the best thing to do."

She stared down at me for a minute, then looked over at the door and then back down at me. "Shyness will never get you anywhere," she stated as she headed to the door, opened it, and went into class as I sat perfectly still and stunned, staring at the door she had just walked through.

I knew, in that moment, that I had learned my first lesson, a life lesson from, as my college president said, "One of the best of the best." This student was for sure a New Yorker. I was for sure a Midwesterner. Not every student in my freshman class had pearls of wisdom for me, but on the whole, they did raise my game. They came from a collection of backgrounds in all shapes, sizes, and persuasions.

My college president was right. Where you put yourself, where you land, where you spend time, whom you spend time with, will dictate and shape your life. I hear my college president's words in my head when I hear my minister speak up at the podium set on our church altar at the center of my grown-up university of choice, my local Presbyterian Church. I learn from sermons that suggest I build my life in bedrock as opposed to the sinking sand. I also hear his words of wisdom as I look around at the congregation. An imperfect group of parishioners for sure. A combination of flawed individuals coming together in a flawed institution.

As I look around at the congregation, as I look around at the collection of real-life curious seekers, I marvel at how they have landed in one of the only institutions where grown-ups and families can go to continue their education. An eclectic gathering of young and old, fancy and everyday, serious and funny, jolly and holy, down to earth and highfalutin. An arrangement of souls, a collection of beings that present a diversity that is rare to be a part of as an adult. Most adults tend to attract others who mirror themselves. They collect others who are raising babies, others who have similar careers, others who have like views.

A church gives you a place to study the way of the Word. Being part of a church gives you a congregation, which, like a student body, delivers a place to continue learning from an assortment of people.

I hear the *clip clop* as I get bossed around in the church kitchen by my fellow worshipers who have been here much longer than I and seem to be able to feed a crowd in record time.

I hear the *clip clop* as I sit in Bible study in my church parlor and hear varying views on what a Bible passage means. They make me think of all those honor students who raised their hand high and proud in my freshman orientation.

As a student at a university, I had to have the discipline to push myself to learn and grow. I had to connect to my curiosity and keep up. As a student at a university, I was in the arena that was all set up for me to take advantage of. As an adult, I find that same arena in the church to continue questioning, pursuing new roles, learning from the learned, and finding compassion and comprehension.

Let me repeat: "Shyness will never get you anywhere." So, do not be shy. Show up.

Show up with all you've got. It is never too late to show up.

Show up with the fear and fascination of a freshman.

Show up, even if you feel those inside are better than you.

Show up at your church doorstep and continue to get educated.

For Further Reflection

Where do you go to find the challenges you need to keep
   growing?
How has God helped to build those experiences?
How has the evolution of that learning been a gift?

Put It into Practice

Do not be shy in your quest to learn. Stay curious as you enter
the doors of worship. When you stand with fellow seekers,
soak up the diversity, the preaching, the collective wisdom,
and various programs that will deliver God's gift of continued
growth.

UNDERSTANDING

George

Let your light so shine before men, that they may see your good works, and glorify your Father which is in heaven.

MATTHEW 5:16 KJV

I really did not want to go in the worst way. It was a very cold morning. I felt like I could have slept for days. I was feeling fat. I had nothing to wear. I could have really used a morning off. I just lay there in my bed thinking, *How can I do it? How can I muster the strength to wake the girls up, then get them dressed, then feed them and get them to church?*

Then guilt started to set in. Then the thought that when you do not want to go, that is when you really should go. *I could really use some inspiration. I would really like some guidance.* Part of my not wanting to get up probably had a lot to do with the fact that I felt stuck in my life. Maybe God would give me a little pep talk through the words of the preacher?

But did I really have to? Did I have to get up and get going?

"Prentiss, Meredith," I yelled, "time to get up and get the get-down feeling, time to get up and get it on! We gotta move out fast."

My procrastinating had meant, even if we hustled, we were going to be late. I still was not feeling it. I still did not want to move. I was still dragging. Meredith, my eight-year-old younger daughter, bounced into my room dressed and ready to go. You have to understand that Meredith, when left to her own devices, dresses...well, she would make Miley Cyrus during her rebellious period look conservative. Today was no exception. She had some kind of midriff on. She would never wear a dress or skirt. Nope, they were not for her. Meredith usually sported tight-fitting leggings topped off with a higher shoe from her dress-up bin. These were heels that she could barely balance on. Not really a showing of her Sunday best. However, I had no energy or time to argue, so off we went.

We tucked into the back door of the church and sat in the back row because church was well under way. Yes, we were late! We had just sat down, disturbing only the back half of the church, when the minister called for all of the children to come to the front of the sanctuary. It was the point in the service where all the kids gathered at the altar with the minister, who would tell them a little story, then off they would go to Sunday school. This morning my Meredith did not want to go up. She would not go up with her sister. She would not go up by herself. *Come on*, I thought, *this is half the reason I came so that Meredith and Prentiss could get a bit of God in them. Help me, Lord!*

After quite a bit of negotiations she agreed to go, but only if I walked her up. So off we marched, right up the center aisle, with everyone watching. Meredith parading in her Sunday splendor, midriff and all. There she was *clip-pity-clopping* her way to the front of the church. If you could not see her get up, you could at least hear it. Subtle we were NOT! I delivered her and her sister to the front of the church, about midway through the children's message.

So as not to cause any more of a ruckus, I scampered off to a side pew up in front, a pew that had only one person I would have to dislodge. The one person was an older gentleman. He politely allowed me to sit beside him at the end of the pew. I had just settled in when Meredith came running to me as opposed to going out with their Sunday school. The polite gentleman once again got up so Meredith could scooch in. I again convinced her to go with the other children. So once again I had to disturb this fine man as we squished by him so that I could take her to her classroom. Then back I came again to occupy my seat next to this kind man who had now been disturbed not once, not twice, but six times by us!

As I got my bearings, I had a few words with God: *God, really? Did you have to make it so very hard upon my arrival? Could you not have made this morning just a bit less about negotiations with my little terrorist and a bit more about the Word? The Word was, after all, what I'm here for. I need you to inspire me. I am looking for you to lift me up. Hello, Jesus? And Meredith? Really? She almost did not make it. Hello?*

As I took my seat, I finally looked up long enough to see what was going on at the front of the church.

No? Really? Could it be? A wedding? A wedding? Taking place in CHURCH? Have you ever even heard of such a thing?

I do not even like weddings when I know the people getting married. These two? Who were they? And why a wedding during Sunday service? I had never heard of such a thing.

Really? OH God why? I should have stayed in bed! This was NOT what I was looking for. A wedding? No. No. No. No. I wanted words. Words for me. Words about me. Spare me.

The kind man's eyes and my eyes met. I smiled; he smiled. We once again faced the front and watched the ceremony. And again the man and I glanced at each other and exchanged smiles.

They finally got to the "I do's." And although I was mighty annoyed, I thought it might be a nice moment to exchange small talk. I turned to the gracious older gentleman whose peace we had disturbed so many times this day and said, "Well, isn't that lovely?"

He responded by locking eyes with mine. He looked square into them and in a bit of a choked-up voice said, "My bride and I exchanged vows here forty years ago. She has passed on and I miss her so much. I always sit in the front of the church, by the door, because since she passed, I have never been able to make it through a whole church service."

At that very moment the minister said, "You may kiss the bride." The whole church erupted.

I wondered what my next move should be. I lived on the East Coast. I went to a very conservative church. This man looked like a stone cold Yankee. And yet...

I wanted to reach out and hug him.

I wanted to grab his hand and hold it tight.

But I did not want to embarrass him or lean in too much. I wanted so much to do the right thing, to lend the right touch, to hold him in just the right way to ease his pain and carry him through. So, I did it...I grabbed this stranger's hand and squeezed it tight. I even had the audacity to tug on it and pull him close. I said to him, in as solid a voice as I could, "I am right here with you and we are going to make it through this." He squeezed back. *Phew*, I thought.

Throughout the rest of the service, I held on tight to him. Sometimes I just held his hand. At other moments, I put my arm around him. We shared the hymnal. We read from one program together. We sang. We stood. We sat. We smiled and nodded with each passing phase of the service.

Right before the last prayer was given, he leaned toward me and said, "I do not know who you are, but I sure am glad you are here."

Our eyes filled with tears as we hugged each other good-bye and left the sanctuary with the rest of the worshipers.

He had made it through the whole service. He had made it through the whole service.

Since that day my family and I always sit with George. He and I hold hands through each Sunday service. When we enter the church, one of the first things my kids say is, "Where is George?" We wait for him and he waits for us.

I thought I was attending church that day with all my messiness and imperfections so that God could help me out, set me straight, move me forward. Well, God did, but just not in the way I'd expected. Well, God did, but in a better way than I could have expected.

I got to be someone's light. My higher-shoe-wearing daughter and I got to be the beacon. My hand held someone's pain and lifted it for just a bit so that he could feel the sun.

Who knew I could be the messenger?

Who knew I could lend the hope?

Who knew I could touch a heart with God's love?

God knew.

God knows.

God can make you more powerful and full of love . . . at just the right place, in just the right pew. So, show up! Show up in all your glory, so that you, too, can be lifted up above your own needs and hopes to bring forward someone else's.

For Further Reflection

Have you ever been a stranger's light?

How did God put you in a place and plug in your light so that
   you and someone else could bask in your wattage?

How was lifting someone out of the darkness a gift?

Put It into Practice

Shine your light in order to be someone's blessing. Focus your light on someone else's pain so that you, with the help of God, can lighten their burden and help them see the sun.

broken plates

*The Lord is close to the brokenhearted and saves those who are
crushed in spirit.*

PSALM 34:18 NIV

The church I grew up in was a big white building on the
main street of our town. Probably not much different than
most Main Street churches across America. Inside, the cavernous three-story church showcased a mixture of dark wood walls
and carved white wood trim around the windows and doors.
The pews, covered in purple textured cushions, kind of wrapped
around the altar in a half circle. And a warm light poured through
the stunning stained-glass windows.

The sanctuary was surrounded by suite after suite of large
meeting rooms. The church unfolded on three different lev-
els. They were rambling floors where one room opened onto
the next. The church, cold in the winter, was equally hot in the
summer. The kitchen was large and industrial, and opened onto
the lower-floor dining room. But the parlor was small and intimate, a quiet place. The choir room was tucked away in a corner, and one walked past the adorable nursery to get to it, which
was always a treat. I loved the winding narrow stairs I had to
crawl up to get to the top floor, where most of the Sunday school
classes were held. Every floor creaked in its own way, giving it a

unique, living voice. Every window opened to a vista that looked out onto a very specific view of my lovely town. Each door had its own way of opening and closing. I had it all memorized. I loved every oddball and rather run-down inch of my funky-dunk church.

When rumor had it that the church leaders were going to tear it down or sell it, to rebuild somewhere on the outskirts of town, I was devastated. That church was where God lived. That was the place where I lived with God. Every cracked piece of paint had God's hand in it. You cannot re-create THAT. You cannot rebuild THAT. But... they did.

Our church packed up and moved to the outskirts of town. We set up in a newly built, mod, simple, well-laid-out, orange-cushioned, practical building with "flexible" rooms. Oh, how I missed my purple, dark wood, and worn white-walled building. Every Sunday of every month, I reminisced about the drafty old Main Street lady love of a church—my church with all its decaying beautiful homeliness. You see, God had shown me the perfection in the rundown. God had made me feel more at home by allowing me to realize the beauty in each chip and dig in the wood and walls. The uneven floor had become my comfort.

My style for living was born in that teardown; and no newfangled flawless fort would ever do. God had drilled into me a love for the worn and the weathered. God had nurtured my love of well-lived-in chic interiors through the beat-up look and feel of my Main Street church.

In my early thirties I had just saved my first chunk of money—like enough-money-for-me-to-buy-a-house money. I went hunting in the only place I had found in my adult life that felt like home to me, the Hamptons. Yes, "those" Hamptons.

My friend Bobby Flay and I rented a place there one summer; and I never wanted to leave.

Needless to say, the first chunk of money I had saved was in no way enough for me to buy much in "those" Hamptons. But that did not stop me. I found the cheapest place on the market. It was owned by an artistic couple who had built it, or more like, gathered it—they had moved two old barns and a butcher shop together, and the combination was this house, my house.

When Bobby came to look at it, he stood in the living room and said, "You are going to tear it down, right?"

Wrong! Nope, not a chance. This house was special to me because it echoed the well-worn wonderfulness of my Main Street church. To me, it was perfection, the one and only house that could and would and should be mine. I was going to embrace the haphazard nature of the joint in a way that would transform it into an enchanting retreat.

Bobby came back a few months later. He got it. He loved it. "Who knew?" he said.

Within months of my revamp, my feathered nest was featured in *Life Magazine*, *Elle Décor*, and *Traditional Home*. Even I was amazed at the fame of my haphazard home.

Not long after I had purchased the house and completed the revamp, I was making a guest appearance on Bobby's television show. We had decided what recipes we would make—who would prepare and chop what and when. But the minute I walked onto the set, Bobby pulled out a gorgeous dinner plate and covered it with a large napkin, then he got out a hammer, and smashed the plate into bits. He looked at me, then at the camera, and said, "My friend Katie is so talented that she can take these pieces of broken plate and turn them into something wonderful."

My life flashed before my eyes. This was live TV, and Bobby Flay had created an impossible challenge for me! I laughed it off and got busy with chopping for the recipe. But in that moment, I saw in Bobby's eyes the pride and utter faith he had in me that I could truly create beauty out of those shards.

God has the same faith in you that Bobby had in me! You can dazzle the world by transforming life's blows, life's throwaway trash, and even your torn-up heart into something powerfully stunning. The bumps, the chips, the flaws that life has dealt are meant to be gathered up and used as fuel for the work of art that is your life.

The run-down beauty that God showed me how to appreciate in the Main Street church of my youth was a great teacher for my grown-up work as a scrappy lifestyle expert and, maybe more important, for my grown-up work of shaping the messes and broken dreams of my life into a well-lived weathered stream of beautiful love.

God has created and designed your talent to overcome, no matter how smashed up your hopes may be. So please know—and yes, have faith—that with God by your side, glory can rise from the most tattered, torn, and even run-down dreams.

For Further Reflection

When have you turned your torn-down dream into a show-
    stopping do-over?
How did God open your eyes to the beauty in the mess?
How were your worn-out, dented dreams a gift?

Put It into Practice

Recognize when you have recycled your defeats into suc-
cesses. Recognize what God is nurturing in you with each
broken experience so that you can realize the beauty in the
struggle and begin to rebuild from there.

a glass heart

For judgment is without mercy to one who has shown no mercy.
Mercy triumphs over judgment.

JAMES 2:13 ESV

My daughter Prentiss went to first grade in a school that I did not much care for. My disdain for this institution started early on in the year. You see, in our family, both my husband and I work and we both parent. At the beginning of the school year, we filled out the necessary forms—name, address, emergency contacts, e-mails—you get the drift. Even though there was room for only one response on most of these lines, we squeezed the information for both myself and my husband onto the form. However, when the school year was getting into its groove—when you tend to get overwhelmed by e-mails—my husband got none and I got tons. Bad choice, because I was not the diligent one of our parenting pair.

We called the school. We wrote e-mails to the teachers. We even stopped into the school office to give them my husband's e-mail address so that they would start including him. Still no e-mails in his in-box.

About one month into the school year, the school hosted an open house. We walked around the room with the other parents. We looked at the students' desks, admired the bulletin boards, their reading area, and their art. We strolled about until it was time for the teacher to make some remarks. Early on in her talk, she said, "Fathers, please note, we do not include you on the e-mail correspondence because we do not want to bother you at work."

WHAT! She must not have meant to say that. I could feel myself getting hot as the hair stood up on the back of my neck.

WHAT? This is an all-girls school in the year 2000. The teacher had just told me and everyone else that my husband's job was far too important to interrupt, but as for the women, the mothers, she would interrupt away. Essentially she was saying that my husband's job was more important than mine.

I managed to calm myself down and get through the rest of the gathering without creating a scene. *I should pick another time to question and try to understand,* I thought. That opportunity came about a month later, when we sat down for a parent-teacher conference.

Her two teachers started to read off my daughter's report card. Man oh man, did my daughter sound fab! But as much as I loved my daughter, I found it hard to believe that she spoke French without my knowing it. My husband and I looked at each other in disbelief!

Apparently she was a math whiz, too. Who knew?...not her mom and dad. "Are you sure this is Prentiss you are talking about?" I questioned.

Yep, they were sure.

Wow! William and I exchanged glances again.

Then, he said, "I just got to stop you. This really does not sound like our Prentiss. Prentiss Corbin?"

They stopped, wrestled a few papers around, and then said, "Oh, our bad. Oops. So sorry. We were reading from the wrong report card."

OKAY?

We listened as they read from the correct report card. Prentiss's correct report card, but we were still in a state of shock. You must understand, this was a small school with small classes on the Upper East Side in New York City. As they wrapped up their report, the teacher said, "Do you have any questions?"

"Just one," I said. "During the orientation tour, you said you did not include fathers on your e-mail notices because you did not want to interrupt them at work. You do realize that mothers work, too? I work. Surely you did not mean that?"

Without missing a beat, she said, "We are a very traditional school."

My head spun. I admit, I was stunned and rendered speechless as I tripped out the door in a bit of a fog of disbelief. I really did not understand this place. I was such a fish out of water.

The following week, I found myself at a get-to-know-you meal with my fellow mothers in Prentiss's class. Again, I felt out of place. I cannot explain it. They were lovely and kind, but just not my people. Perhaps this was because I already had a chip on my shoulder about the whole place? I'm just not sure, but I could not wait for the dinner to be over. As the other moms praised the school and the teachers, I found my resentment growing. I stiffened with each new glorifying story.

We were given a little package upon departing the gathering. It was a lovely little box. When I got home and opened it, I found a carved crystal heart inside about the size of the palm of my hand. It was almost like a prism where the sun would enter and a rainbow of light would come through the other side. I really didn't care for it, and that made perfect sense to me since I did not care for the school. I felt, I would not have a place for it anywhere in my home. Just like the school was not a home for my family.

We moved on from that school, but no matter how hard I tried, I could not move on from that crystal prism heart. I placed it in the trash pile many times, only to find it back in my daughter's room. I asked Prentiss to give it as a birthday gift (yes, I do re-gift), but that, too, never happened. At one point it fell off her nightstand. I looked down with glee, hoping it had shattered in a zillion pieces and I would be able to sweep it away with all the bad memories from that school. But alas there it was, that whole heart with not even a chip. *UGHHH.*

My younger daughter, Meredith, went through a spell when she was a little over four years old where she was having a really hard time sleeping through the night. During this period, she would make it most of the night, but never quite the WHOLE night. I would hear little footsteps tiptoeing down the hall. Then, she would pull away my covers and slide in right next to me. We were not that family who believed in kids sleeping in our bed, and I really had tried everything to get her to make it through in her own bed till morning.

One night, Prentiss was helping me put her younger sister to sleep. As we neared the end of our bedtime ritual that culminates in our nightly prayers, Meredith's tears started to flow. "PLEASE, can I sleep with you? PLEASE? I get too scared. PLEASE?"

All of a sudden, Prentiss lit up. "Hold on," she said. She ran out of the room and came back clutching something in her hand. She placed it gently in Meredith's hand. Before she let it go, she looked Meredith right in the eye and said, "Hold this tight. It will stay with you all night and make you strong. When you feel frightened, hold on tighter."

Meredith smiled and reluctantly quieted down with that stubborn crystal heart buried in her clutch. Meredith slept through that night. She slept through that entire night in her own bed, under her own sheets, with her head on her own pillow. The next morning, with daylight blazing, she ran into my room sporting a very self-satisfied look on her face. She let the heart fall from her hand in order to give me a big hug of relief. She had done it. She had moved on. We never again revisited the stress and strain of all those sleepless nights with little Meredith trying to escape her room.

I picked up that heart and had a heart moment of my own, a moment when my heart sighed and allowed a few fond memories from that school to roll through my mind. Memories of how our daughter was able to go to one of the best museums in the world for art class because it was steps away from the school's front door. Memories of how our beloved minister's wife got to sit with our daughter at least three days a week because she was one of the art teachers. Memories of how we never had to argue or focus on what our daughter wore because the school required a uniform. Memories of how it was at that school that our daughter began learning Mandarin, a language she still studies eight years later.

Thank You, God, for easing my anger.

No matter how complicated the challenge may be. When you allow your own light, flawed with all its judgment and self-centeredness and fears, to run through the prism of God's love, which is as pure and devoted and similar to the deepness of sisterly love, you will be able to see the rainbow of colors in the good and in the bad, so that your heart can open and heal.

That morning, I gingerly placed the crystal heart back on its shelf in our home, right where it belonged.

For Further Reflection

When have you looked beyond your judgment in order to see
    something good?

How did God help shift your focus from the judgment to appre-
    ciation and understanding?

How was this shift in perspective a gift?

Put It into Practice

See all the different colors in the spectrum when you are form-
ing your opinions. Be open to allowing God to shift your perspective in order to better see the whole of a situation or a
person.

a GPS

The heart of man plans his way, but the Lord establishes his steps.

PROVERBS 16:9 ESV

I was feeling a bit panicked. Maybe even a bit manic. We had just accepted an offer on our family home in Connecticut. We were to close in one month's time. As in, move out in thirty days. The buyers needed it all to happen quickly.

This was a home we had lived in for the last decade of our lives. Which, by the by, was the longest I had ever lived in any one place since leaving my parents' home over thirty years earlier.

Our faithful Connecticut home was a big old Betty of a house. She was a grand dame. She was an old rambling lady. From the minute I walked through the front door, I felt like she was an old friend. She felt like the best keeper of my secrets. It was a home I had brought back to life. It sheltered, nurtured, and breathed life into our budding family.

It was a disorienting thought to leave this home. Yes, I wanted to sell. We were ready to move on. But I ached to bring this lovely, gracious, spacious ship with me. This house with its creaky floors and sunken ceilings was part of our family, an intimate string that seemed woven into our daily comings and goings.

Thirty days. Thirty days. We had to move out in thirty days, and I did not even know where to begin. I could not even gather my thoughts let alone my belongings.

My soul somehow seemed embedded in this home's very walls. I was dying to sell the house. The old gal had been on the market for one year. We were downright gleeful to have a buyer. But where to now? Where would my heart land? How could we replace such a gem? Such a gallant soldier in our everyday battles of family life? How could I walk away from a house that had become my friend?

It is just a house. Just a house? But I am a house person. I could not imagine shedding this skin. Maybe, if I knew what my next suit of armor was going to look like, it would be easier. If I knew exactly what greener pastures were awaiting us, it would seem doable. However, I was not really sure where that was. Not even really sure what part of the country it would be in. Part of me wanted to return to the sunny shore of LA. Part of me wanted to return to my Midwestern roots. Part of me wanted the bright lights of Manhattan.

I know. I know. Seems all a bit too carefree for a mother of two, with the older child about to start high school. All responsible caregivers have a plan. A solid, good, thought-out, wise road map of how and where to raise their young. My head and heart were spinning. But I did not dare let on to my posse of four. I was steadfast that this was right...a must migration if we were to move forward.

I yearned for some sense of what and where our next fort would be. Surely, if I could stake a claim and wrestle some new abode to the ground, my anxiety would subside. And what is so wrong with that? Like I said, I am a house person. My home is my security, my anchor. *Yes, that is it!* All would be well if I just *knew* that our next home was waiting with open arms.

Then, a call came out of the blue... from a Realtor I had met in my many travels to my parents' Midwestern town. She sent me a link to a home that was right in the crosshairs of the houses owned by my sister, my brother, and my mother and father.

It seemed like another beauty of a home, old and in disrepair. It appeared homely yet heavenly. My breath slowed for the first time in forty-eight hours since we had received the offer on our house. The best part? We could afford it. Maybe not the fixing-up part, but we could afford to purchase it. The rest, well, hopefully that could come in time. Homes like this do *not* come up for sale often in this popular Michigan college town.

I was struck with more panic. *I better get there! I better see it.*

It was 9 a.m. when I said to my husband, "I got to go."

"Go where?" he asked.

"To the house," I responded.

"What house?" he asked.

"The house. I think maybe it is where we are supposed to go live," I explained.

"Slow down," he cautioned. "Let's at least get through inspections."

"Nope. I think we have to move quickly," I insisted. (Again I told you I was manic.)

"Let's hold tight," my husband reasoned. "You cannot just fly out on a whim. We do not even know that this is where we want to be."

"Yep, yep, I know it seems crazy, but I have to move. I have to jump," I said.

The next thing I knew, he indulged me by looking for a plane ticket. They were all far too expensive for such a frivolous impulse.

But I would not be dissuaded. "I will drive," I stated conclusively.

"Drive? By yourself?" he asked. "That is at least a whole day's journey."

"Yep, well, it has to be done," I said knowingly as I began throwing clothes in my bag.

My husband knew better than to try to stop me, but he did add, "Might I just remind you that we do have a 'not to be missed' meeting in two days?"

"I know," I said. "I am going to zip there and back. I will drive all night if I have to." I bolted out the front door and onto the open road.

Two hours-4 hours-8 hours-11 hours later I arrived at my parents' home. I met the Realtor, and the house, and it did not disappoint. It could never be a substitute for my Betty, but it would be a fine next act. The problem was, it was in way worse shape than I had expected. The price was too high for the amount of work that would have to be done, and the owners were not budging.

In order to make it in time for my "not to be missed" meeting, I had to turn right around and head home. It was in those long hours driving alone in my car that I realized perhaps I had let my fear drive me to Michigan. My fear of the unknown, my need for control, had caused me to head my car in a direction that would force a conclusion of our next scene.

Hour 1-Hour 3-Hour 4-It seemed that my iPhone traffic app, Waze, was directing me to go off the main drag. *Why?* I thought. There was no sign of a slowdown. Nope, I was not going to listen to Waze. I was going to stay the course. But Waze is rarely wrong. It always steers me in the right direction. We have a saying in our family: "Do not doubt the Waze." This time it was tough to trust because it seemed like it was smooth sailing on the interstate. There was no sign of a traffic jam anywhere to be found. But if Waze said so, I better follow, so off I turned. The road seemed to go in the exact opposite direction.

Hour 5. *Wow, what a road*, I thought. It curved, it winded, it rambled; it was hilly and gorgeous. It doled out one more breath-taking vista after another. Farms like I had never seen with cows grazing and the sun blazing flew past my car windows. This was God's country like I had never seen before. *Wow, thank you, Waze, for trekking me through this masterpiece of a landscape.* I was blissed out.

At Hour 5½ I was cresting yet another hill with yet another mesmerizing view when it hit me . . . Why was I so willing to give up control to Waze? I was so sure it knew best that I disregarded my own instinct and put my directional fate in its hand. But when my loving God threw me a curve ball in the form of a move, I pounced on the situation with the need to wrestle the outcome and the answers to the ground.

Hour 6. The divergent road delivered me back to the main drag of the highway right in front of dead-stopped traffic. I merged on and raced off toward home, having avoided what could have been hours long delay.

Hour 7. My moves were God's moves. My time was God's time. God would guide me and my family, at the right time, to the right place, without my having to force a thing. I needed to sit back, breathe in, and have faith.

Hour 8. My husband called to tell me our deal back home had fallen through.

Hour 9. I had learned, yet again, that I was not in the driver's seat...no matter what house I lived in or where I lived.

Hour 10. God would find me the Waze home. God would always deliver me to the right road that would lead me to where I needed to go at the perfect time, if I could just dull my manic moods long enough to feel, to see, and breathe.

Hour 11. I was back home with a settled heart. I knew I was meant to be a mere passenger in this next rite of passage.

For Further Reflection

When have you felt panic about a journey you were on because you did not know where you are headed?

How was God with you on that journey and what was the lesson?

How did the lesson in that journey turn into a gift?

Put It into Practice

Trust God through the discomfort of the journey. Put your faith in God that the road you are to take will become clear. Put your fate in God's hands when you need to start anew, knowing that He will be there to guide you every step of the way.

a temper

For all have sinned and fall short of the glory of God.

ROMANS 3:23 ESV

A wonderful woman I admired who ran a big business once told me to drop a pencil when I felt frustrated with an employee. She explained that you should always take a beat. When her instinct was to lash out, she said she would drop a pencil. By the time she bent down and grabbed it up and then stood back up, she would have a different point of reference. She said that simple act always lowered the temperature in the room. By physically moving away from the moment, she claimed, it would literally give her the patience she needed to respond more thoughtfully.

Another fine female friend of mine was about to celebrate her sixtieth wedding anniversary. I asked her what her secret was. How did she manage to stay happily married all those years? "Sweetie," she said with confidence, "sometimes it pays to be slightly hard of hearing."

Then there was the 80-20 rule that I once had a therapist explain to me. She taught me that a good way to deal with people is to limit your expectations by knowing that it is rare to find someone who can deliver 100 percent of the time. "Your job, as a leader," she elaborated, "is to discover how to aid them the other twenty percent of the time."

I am a fighter. I enter a room ready for battle.

I was raised in a combative household. Rarely did or does anyone in my family avoid confrontation. A shrinking violet I am not. I appeased my concerns over my temperament by applying adjectives like "fierce," "determined," "driven." As an adult, my employees were in the line of fire of my fierce manner. Now, please note I do not mean to overexaggerate. I had good relations with my team for the most part. But there were moments when my need to win, to push the business forward, would cause me to come down hard on anyone who I felt was not doing their job or not supporting my business goals.

I was collecting strategies on how and when to call my employees to the mat. I knew, I still know, this was an area where I had to improve in order to have a productive, thriving, supportive work environment and life. However, my obsessive controlling and suspicious nature continued to be my worst enemy.

Dropping a pencil? PLEASE! I thought.

Hard of hearing? I hear everything in every part of my workshop. My employees often say, "How did you hear that?"

80/20 rule? What about giving 150 percent?

I wanted better. I wanted more for my great staff. I wanted to be the boss who they talked about when discussing whom they learned and grew from. I wanted the Workshop to be that stop on their career trajectory that they felt had taught them the most. Perhaps this all comes from being a girl who was raised in the Midwest, where being nice was paramount.

Or maybe my guilt over not being a good enough boss stemmed from the fact that, like most women, I was raised knowing that I had to be sweet, kind, and nice no matter the circumstances. I was raised to believe it was important that everyone *liked me*. My gut knew I had to develop a better way to manage people no matter how I rationalized my behavior.

I am embarrassed to admit I have made people cry when critiquing their work. I have approved production schedules so grueling that team members have broken down from exhaustion. My manner at times was so intimidating that some were afraid to talk with me.

I have a heavy heart when I think of those moments.

Many times, in those moments, I wanted to jump out, jump off. I wanted to retreat to a simpler existence where I did not have to lead anyone, where I did not have to be in a position of authority with the ability to hurt anyone. Clearly, leading with positivity was not my strength.

On one such occasion, I walked away from the set to try to regain my composure. My beloved cameraman and director followed after me as I fought back tears of frustration due to my overreaction to some coworkers who I felt had done less than acceptable work.

Van, my cameraman, put his arm around me and pointed to two other cameramen. "You see him and her?" he said.

"Yes." I nodded.

He pointed to a few of the chefs working on our show and said, "Do you see those two?"

"Yes," I said.

He turned me in another direction. He pointed and said, "Do you see her, him, him, her, and him? They are all here because of you. I know this is not easy for you, but we are all here because of you. He can eat tonight. She can have a cocktail. She will be able to buy a new pair of shoes. You got this, Katie. You got this."

I walked right back in front of the camera.

I had failed at finding a calmer path just a few minutes earlier, but I would go back and try to do better, knowing that I must try harder to change my less-than-gentle manner.

Dropping a pencil seemed too simple. Acting like I was hard of hearing was almost impossible. The 80-20 rule was not enough.

But just because I failed and failed again did not mean I was a failure. It did not have to be the end.

The Bible reveals to us that King David broke half the commandments. Elijah suffered burnout. John Mark was slow with his devotion. Peter denied Christ on more than one occasion. Paul was an enemy of the early Christian Church.

My failure did not mean I had failed unless I let it. I had to have faith that if I gave my missteps and defeats to God, God would continue to guide me in my struggles.

When I think of bright moments in my career, I think of my team member who moved on to write several DIY books of her own. I then remember another who went on to a high position with a competitor. I marvel at others who became distinguished decorators, window decorators, theater dressers, and furniture designers. My point is, I loved watching my former employees fly. I hope I had a hand in the heights they reached.

With each mountain I see them climb, I make a humble promise . . . to do better with the next talented person God sends my way.

For Further Reflection

What have you done when you discovered the places in your life where self-improvement was needed?

How has God helped deliver to you the messages and tools you needed to practice and move toward a better way?

How has this better way of living or thinking about things or improved habits been a gift?

Put It into Practice

Gather, test, and implement tools that will help you rise above your shortcomings. Notice along the way when God presents you with the tools you need to get you closer toward a transformation.

LOVE

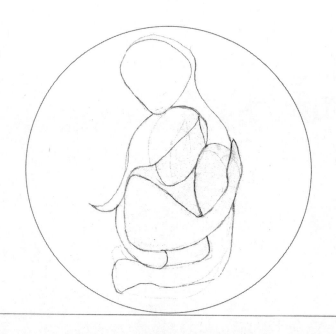

long arms

Set your minds on things that are above, not on things that are on earth.

COLOSSIANS 3:2 ESV

I forgot to get married and have a baby. In my childhood playrooms, I would wrap an apron around my waist and stand at my little wooden kitchen and prepare the wooden painted food. On the playground, I always went to the play structures and got busy putting together some semblance of a house while everyone else was climbing higher and higher. My favorite part about playing with Barbies? Putting them in an apron, setting their table, styling up their apartment, and selecting their babies. Give me all of it, a family, a home, all of it!

I would do stand-up comedy routines in between the takes of my TV show about how I was a wife waiting to happen. I would lament how I had been so busy pursuing a career that taught people, wives, and homemakers how to manage their home and family that I had forgotten to build one myself.

I resented my career deeply. I felt it had kept me from the one thing I wanted most in life...*a family*. So, I did something supremely self-destructive. I did not renew my TV show contract with Lifetime Television.

My agent screamed at me, "You cannot do this! Do you know

how lucky you are to have a hit TV show? Do you know how hard it is to get a TV show? Let alone a top-rated one? Listen to me!"

"I quit," I said.

For so long, I'd poured all workaholic me into my job and now nothing. Wow, was it depressing! What had I done? Clearly my impulsive move to leave my career behind was not at all the answer. So I quickly partnered with my agents to get back to work before the shine of my successful Lifetime TV show wore off. We scored with a Food Network and HGTV gig. That one ended before it really even began. The beauty of my profession that I had taken for granted was really sinking in. Then, we landed a Style Network gig. That, too, was canceled after a few seasons. Oh, how I missed the creative discussions that I had so cavalierly begrudged. I even kind of missed the long hours. I for sure missed the steady paycheck. Finally, I landed another show on A&E Network. I went back to work every day on that job with deep gratitude.

One day while I was taping and performing my truly pain-induced routine of a wife-waiting-to-happen, a suit, a big wig, a muckety-muck from A&E said, "I have a guy for you."

Doubtful, I thought.

Early on, my dating life had been a series of monogamous relationships. Yep, the minute I kissed someone, I was theirs for life! As a result, boy after boy, man after man, went RUNNING! I was always the one broken up with and never the one doing the breaking up. I spent more nights on friends' and families' couches nursing my broken heart than anyone I knew. To protect my aching heart, I developed a self-defensive habit. As my budding relationships unfolded, I would start a running list in my head of reasons why my current suitor was not THE ONE. My dating scars had evolved into a pattern of having a compiled list on-the-ready so that I could be the first to end the courtship.

Reluctantly, I agreed to a date (these were my A&E bosses arranging the setup, after all). A foxy man named William came to my door. Once again, within weeks, I was about to dismiss yet another relationship due to his many shortcomings.

You see:

Number one, his arms were way too long for his body. Number two, he seemed to have too many names (Will, Willy, Bill, Boo). Number three, I had to spend many hours hearing about his accomplishments, which included being able to hold his breath longer than any Navy SEAL. Did I mention he was younger than I was?

That evening, as we were parting ways, I was secretly plotting my exit strategy, when he reached for me and pulled me close by wrapping his long arms around me. I reluctantly softened into the hug. I realized that he could wrap his limbs around me almost twice. I found there was something soothing in the security of his lengthy grip.

That moment was the beginning of a life together filled with glorious exaggerations that made everything seem possible. It was the beginning of a potpourri of diverse friends (each of whom called him by a different name). It was the start of a journey with a multitalented youthful partner to explore all of life's possibilities.

It was in all of my husband's earthly imperfections that I found a heavenly home. One year to the date of our first date, on Mother's Day no less, I gave birth, with my new husband by my side, to our older daughter, Prentiss Crocket Corbin.

It took me throwing away my career in order for me to connect with the deeper meaning in my work. Throwing it away literally and figuratively, in order for me to understand how it grounded me. In order to prepare me—a whole, happy me, a grateful me—to be present, to see, to recognize, to notice, to be rooted in the right stuff to be tuned in enough . . . to recognize my husband.

God's timing during my journey toward properly placed priorities was divine.

Through my stubborn, self-sabotaging actions, God brought me to a place of sincere understanding of how my career fit into my life. This understanding led to a place physically and emotionally that allowed me to find and recognize God's next blessing. The blessing of understanding that a man with long arms could fit into my life.

Trust that no matter what direction your self-defeating self might take you, God will use it to move you closer toward your potential.

For Further Reflection

How have your missteps been a blessing in shaping your priorities?

How has God's grace shined through your missteps and strengthened your discernment?

How has the comprehension that came from your stumbles been a gift?

Put It into Practice

Value the realizations of the heavenly qualities of your life experiences and your loves that have come from the mistaken directions you have gone in your life. Know that when you walk with God, your blunders may very well be none other than blessings that can teach you how to get closer to your dreams.

an incubator

And he awoke and rebuked the wind and said to the sea, "Peace! Be still!" And the wind ceased, and there was a great calm.

MARK 4:39 ESV

I gave birth to a premature baby. Our little Prentiss was born two months early. How is it possible that I, who had waited and waited for a baby my whole life, could have given birth early? How is it possible that I, who could not wait to hold my baby in my arms, was terrified to hold my baby because she weighed all of three pounds and looked like a bird who would break when touched? And how would it be possible to endure the pain of driving home from the hospital while she remained there, in an incubator, with tubes keeping her alive?

I am a workaholic. I had planned to get back to work as soon as possible after my delivery. I had a new show on A&E, a new book on the shelves, a product line to design, a *New York Times* syndicated column to write. However, it seemed God had other plans for me, because I spent the next several weeks in the neonatal intensive care unit.

Instead of creating a new season of episodes, I learned the art of kangarooing. Kangarooing is what you do with a premature baby by holding it close to you between your breasts in order for your body heat to nurture the baby's growth. Every hour of every day, I held my daughter close. I sang to her. I talked to her. All the while, begging God and begging my wee baby to make it.

During the times when the nurses were holding and checking on my baby, I was pumping barely flowing breast milk, hoping there would be enough to feed my daughter through a tube. She had not yet developed the sucking instinct. The entire time praying that she would someday . . . come home.

About a week earlier, my doctor had ordered bed rest for me. Now, that job, being on bed rest, I was not so good at. My forty-year-old, self-centered, workaholic self got a quick, fast, glorious lesson in the art of priorities. Nothing else now mattered in my life except the health of my darling daughter.

Three weeks later, we brought our baby home. What before our baby would have seemed inconceivable, the next six months . . . I did nothing but bond with my baby. I was slowly learning the art of mothering.

After a glorious six months, I did pick up the phone to once again reconnect with my career.

I still struggle with my busy schedule. I still fight to find the balance of my busy career and the role of mother. Each choice has been richly informed by the transforming terror of those first three weeks.

Rarely do I not find a way to choose to enjoy my daughter.

Each moment with her has been made that much sweeter knowing how close we came to never knowing her.

Every time she flashes me a look with her loving eyes, I know my cannonball journey into motherhood may have been the only way that I would have slowed down long enough . . . paid attention long enough . . . to feel like I'd earned it, and thus my heart was open to receive such a stunning gift.

So remember to pay attention to what God is delivering to you during your downtime. Note how you are transformed during life's shutdowns.

Pay attention to the insights and qualities that develop or surface during these periods. Because God's schedule is always on time, we must take stock of the heavenly transformation that can happen when our earthly clock seems to tick tock to a different beat...than when you are seated in God's waiting room.

For Further Reflection

How have you been slowed by events in your life long enough
to experience grace?
How has this shift allowed God to deliver to you new habits
and rituals and roles that enrich your life?
How has this timing been a gift?

Put It into Practice

Stop, be still, so you can breathe in your life lessons. Turn your
impatience into a steady calm so that you can fully receive the
goodness God is sending your way.

a gypsy

*Above all, keep loving one another earnestly, since love covers a
multitude of sins.*

1 PETER 4:8 ESV

I have an older sister named Lynnie. And growing up, I was not
the best of sisters. We had a sibling rivalry that could rival the
best of them. She was smart and interested in engines and planes.
She was curious about the details and the interworking of most
things. I was quick-witted and interested in people, and how to
make them laugh and feel comfortable. She was a real classic
beauty and I was, well, cute. Really, in almost all ways we were as
opposite as they come. She is neat and I am messy. She is a book-
worm and I love art. Growing up, she was a dancer and I was,
well, I am not really sure, but not a dancer. She was Felix to my
Oscar. I was her yin to my yang.

You get the picture.

This makes it all seem like we fit just perfectly together...

But when we were growing up, that was really very often not
the case. We fought. We screamed. We did all we could to be the
brightest in the room, to make very sure our individual lights out-
shined the other. It seemed quite natural to me to be at odds with,
and the opposite of, my bossy awkward older sister. She did not
want to be anything like me nor I her.

There were moments in time where our varying strengths did work well together. She would navigate us through airports when we were young, like a drill sergeant, while my mind wandered. As I tried to figure out the various relationships of the people in the waiting area, she would deliver us to the gate on time and insist we sit in the back of the plane because that was the safest place to be in the event of a crash, while I would be the one who could charm the gate agent into securing those seats for us. Lynn was the one to organize, write, and direct the plays we performed, while my hammy nature would bring down the house. Boss Lady Lynn started the fudge company that we launched from our basement, but I was the sales leader whose door-to-door sales calls brought in the most dough-ray-me.

Please know these simpatico examples were only momentary. The majority of our relationship was adversarial at best and downright savage at its worst.

Until one morning my tortured love for her provided me with a sensation that I had never experienced before nor would I experience very often again in my life. Every fall, on Halloween, Ottawa Elementary School hosted a parade, which took place in the school gymnasium. All the grades would line up and march around in one big circle as parents and teachers looked on. They would *Ooh* and *Ahh* from the sidelines. I was in fourth grade and my sister was in fifth. That year was going to be a great march for me, because my costume was killer. I could not wait to show it off. You see, that was the year of the gypsy. Even my hypercool cousin Kassie was going to be a gypsy. My mom said I could be one, too. I was lucky because my mom was that mom who allowed me to go big on this ghoulish holiday. This was odd because she despised the trick-or-treating part, but she was always supportive during the costume preparations.

That year was no exception. She took me to Jo-Ann Fabrics and we picked out the most amazing electric blue paisley print fabric. Next, we found some pink fringe that picked up some of the pink in the paisley print to trim the whole getup. My mom sewed through the night a skirt, a matching shawl, and a headdress. I had big hoop clip-on earrings and a few bold necklaces that finished off the look. Because it was Northern Michigan and chilly in October, she bought me a golden turtleneck to wear under the shawl. It was perfect!

Lynn had decided that this year she would be a nurse. For some reason, she had decided to get a mail-order costume, which was odd. We had often thought how lucky we were not to have to buy costumes. We had often discussed that manufactured getups just seemed flat to us compared to the ensembles we would concoct with the help of our mother. As I suspected, when the costume arrived, it did not have the same depth as Lynn's previous homemade Halloween attire. I kept that thought to myself even though I had a feeling Lynn felt the same way.

The day of the parade, the doorbell rang. Both Lynn and I galloped to the door all dolled up in our Halloween best. Me the homemade gypsy, and Lynn the store-bought nurse. Our beloved grandmother, Mom Brown, was on the other side of the door. We were both excited to debut our outfits.

She looked at me and threw up her hands in delight saying, "What a fine gypsy girl you are." Then her eyes fell on Lynn. It took her a moment before she said, "Now, Lynnie, tell me who you are supposed to be? I am not really sure what you are."

There was silence.

No, she did not say that? Yes, she did say that.

Time stood still for a minute.

My heart sank.

Lynn's bottom lip began to quiver, that slowly turned into all-out sobbing. I believe in that moment Lynn's suspicions were confirmed. Her store-bought costume did not measure up. It was more than she could bear. And as it turned out, it was more than I could bear, because in that moment, in the calmest of voices and in the most convincing tone, I said, "Well, thank goodness, because I have been wanting to wear your costume from the minute I saw it, Lynn. Do you think you would ever let me be the nurse and you be the gypsy?"

Almost immediately the crying stopped. Lynn looked at me hopefully. "You really want to be a nurse?" she asked.

"In the worst way," I said.

And with that the deal was struck. My beloved gypsy costume in return for her healed heart.

I felt a sensation during this exchange I'd never experienced before. You must understand I had heard my sister cry dozens and dozens of times in my nine years as her younger sibling, but I had never felt the need or the desire to sacrifice in order to relieve her pain. Never. In fact, quite the opposite was true. But in that moment, standing in my front hall, in that first decade of my young life, I was graced with compassion in a way that I had never known before.

The next thing I remember, Lynn was all gypsyed up and I was a walking white nurse. I think I was more stunned than anyone at my compulsive selfless act. It was the first time in my life that God had blessed me with the impulse to heal and love and have empathy for someone who most of the time felt like my enemy.

We posed for pictures . . . all in a row with my cool older gypsy cousin. My sister in my paisley print, fringed gypsy look and me as a caregiving nurse.

As I look back, it was the perfect costume for me that year. It was the year my heart grew, while dressed as the nurse who helped heal my sister's heartache.

Now I know this is a simple, rather undramatic, short, almost meaningless exchange to most. But to me it was such a powerful, moving instant, because . . . something way wiser than myself led me to LOVE.

As we pranced around the gym, because I was a class behind my sister, I had a perfect view of Lynn just ahead of me in perfect gypsy fashion and the bystanders who cheered as she passed them by.

This was my first powerful moving instant when the Holy Spirit took over to allow my young earthly soul to experience the depth and complexity of Christian Love. As I passed by the school staff and heard the familiar Halloween *Oohs* and *Ahhs*, my somewhat disappointed heart thought, *If they only knew what I know, they would be marveling at my momentary healing nature that matches my costume perfectly.*

For Further Reflection

On what occasion has your ability to love someone surprised you?

How did your actions, in that moment, seem so unlike you that it could have only been God working through you?

How was your loving role, in that moment, a gift?

Put It into Practice

When the Spirit moves you, go ahead and give up something you love, for someone you love, and watch the new heights of love God's transformation takes you to.

a parfait

Then Jesus told him, "Because you have seen me, you have believed;
blessed are those who have not seen and yet have believed."

JOHN 20:29 NIV

On my eighth birthday, my mother was not at home. She
had given birth to my brother the night before my big day.

She was a mom who made you feel pretty special on your birthday. She would always have a cake that was the culmination of
much discussion and design talk. An after-school birthday with
a theme and an activity to match. The celebration always ended
with the presentation of said cake.

Because she had been in the hospital for a few days, we had not
had time to do our usual planning. However, the party was still
on for that afternoon.

I arrived home from school that day with my posse of friends.
One of our babysitters, Cindy, greeted us at the front door. Yes, I
liked her, but would she know how to make the party fun?

Where was my mom?

Upon our arrival, Cindy led us all into our living room. Hanging in the center of the room was a piñata. I had never seen one
before. It was a rare and exotic party prop back in those days. I
knew what it was. I knew we had to take the sticks that she had
laid out and hit it until we cracked it. Then the candy would fall to

the ground. Sadly, I was not the one to land the strike to cause all the candy to fall.

Where was my mom?

You see, I spent a lot of my childhood feeling a bit lonely. I felt like an outsider most of the time. Even at my own birthday party, my friends often felt like strangers. I would, more times than not, feel like I was having an out-of-body experience. I would feel like I was just moving through the exercise of being.

I was really somehow just observing as I walked through my days.

This party, in particular, was really hitting me hard and made me pull back into myself even more than usual. Yep, I was a lonely outsider at my own ball.

Where was my mom?

My eight-year-old self did not know much. I did not know how or why, but I did know that when I thought or sort of daydreamed about God, I felt less alone, less distant. Somehow, I felt calm... almost like a blanket was around me to keep me safe and cozy and full. Dare I say, my eight-year-old self felt whole when I focused on God's love? For this birthday I needed God big time.

Where was my mom?

A new baby brother, whose arrival had disrupted, at this moment I felt, ruined my birthday.

A babysitter running the show.

A piñata full of candy, none of which landed in my bag.

Right then and there I took a moment and prayed. *God, please be with me*, I mumbled as I breathed that comforting thought in.

Finally... drum roll, please... it was time for the cake. When I told Cindy the time had come to light the candles and gather everyone for the singing of the song, Cindy said, "No. No. Your mom did not say anything about a cake."

"What?" I asked.

"There is *no* cake," she stated in an almost cruel matter-of-fact way.

I fought back tears.

Where was my MOM?

"But," Cindy said, "open the freezer. I think she left something for dessert in there." I was grateful to be able to turn away, because my eyes were beginning to fill and I did not want Cindy to see my tears. I knew she was working hard to make it all seem special.

Where was my mom?

I opened the door. As the mist from the freezer cleared, I saw a blur of bright colors. More frost drifted away. There they stood in all their glory. Six tall glasses filled with layer after layer of brightly colored rainbow sherbet, cake pieces, and fruits.

"Parfaits," Cindy said. "Your mother made you parfaits."

I had never seen or heard of a parfait. *WOW!* The colored stripes matched the stripes in the piñata. They were each topped with the most amazing little paper umbrellas, the kind that you got when you ordered a fancy restaurant drink.

I giggled with glee. They were so beautiful. I was in awe.

My mom, the mother of my new brother, the one who made sure my babysitter was on the ready, the one who searched out an exotic birthday activity, where was she? My mom was right there.

My mom, the one who brought all those colors and combined them with all her love to create something so much more glamorous than a cake to end my fete with a bang... My mom was with me at that party.

Her love was with me through all her preparations that culminated in those long, tall, colorful, over-the-top desserts.

No, I could not see her. But I could feel her. My mom's love, that motherly love, was as deep and strong and steadfast and so much like God's love, was there with me at that party.

If I, if we, can just take in that knowledge and have faith and hold on through all the cold, blinding frost, we will realize we are not alone.

If I, if we, can hold on to that knowledge and have faith that God's motherly love will always enwrap us, it will get us through in ways and with colors more brilliant than we could have ever imagined.

I was blinded by what I could not see. Then I was soothed by what I could. Who knew exotic piñatas and parfaits could have made me feel so special and so loved on my birthday?

My mom's love knew.

God's love knows.

For Further Reflection

When was there a time when you felt lonely and doubtful?
How did God take that doubt-filled loneliness and show you
that He was walking right there with you?
What gifts did God send you to help you realize He was present
the whole time?

Put It into Practice

Stop, breathe, notice, and reflect on the signs that are right in
front of you that prove you are not alone. Take stock in the way
God's love surrounds you in so very many ways. Wait and be
still as the frost settles so you can take in the motherly love of
God hugging you tight.

a seashore

Call to me and I will answer you, and will tell you great and hidden things that you have not known.

JEREMIAH 33:3 ESV

I was just getting started. But somehow, I felt I was getting too old. Too old to marry, that is. And too old to start a family. I was in my late thirties. I had just suffered yet another heartbreaking breakup. All three of my siblings (two younger than I) had gotten married. Two had babies, and one was well on their way to giving birth.

When I walked up to members of my family, they would be talking in hushed tones, and stopped the minute they saw me. It seemed they were feeling just a bit sorry for me and discussed the trajectory of my single life quite often among themselves.

When our family would gather for overnight reunions, I would be given sheets to sleep on the couch while my married siblings would be granted a bedroom. It was ingrained in my Midwestern self that marriage and family and house and home meant you had arrived into adulthood successfully. Clearly, I was not there and there was no sign of me nearing the goal that I was taught would complete me.

I was working nonstop and loving every moment of that.

But I still wanted a home and a family of my own. I wanted to be settled, yet I was alone. I was spending the summer on the other coast. I was living in LA, but working so many days in New York City that I decided to rent a place there for the summer. I found a place in a little town right on the Atlantic a few hours' drive from the city. It seemed I could have the best of both worlds there. I could have a real old-fashioned beach summer on the weekends while still being able to work in the city during the week.

Well, for me and this little town, it was love at first sight. It reminded me of the town I grew up in on the shores of Lake Michigan. I felt at home the minute my bare feet hit the sandy beaches. I felt at home in that place like I never had in my adult life. As the summer rolled along, my heart filled with dread at the thought of leaving it at the end of August to return to Los Angeles. Then it hit me: *Why leave? Why go?*

I had saved a bit of money. Not a lot of money. But what a good investment it would be to put my dough into real estate. But wait. Really? Buy a house as a single girl? I know it seems obvious now, but back then not so much.

I did not know anyone like me who had purchased a house by herself for herself. I could count on one hand the number of single women I knew who were homeowners. It simply was rare back in the day.

I found a beat-up, charming, eclectic home that I could actually afford. Even though it was not the way I ever thought I would buy a home, it was on Butter Lane ... I mean, come on.

There was something overwhelming and something a bit sad about the prospect. But there was also something thrilling, exciting, exhilarating about the idea that I, me, alone could make this dream come true for myself. A home of my own, in a place, a town, a coast just right for me.

But still, maybe I should wait till I have a family to fill it with, and a partner to help bear the burden and the joys. Oh, what to do?

I was getting lots of pressure from the broker to make up my mind. It was the cheapest house in the entire town. It had the wear and tear to show for it. It was quite a fixer-upper, which was all I could afford and exactly what I wanted.

I took myself for a walk on the beach. I sat myself down between a few sand dunes, and prayed:

Please God,
If it is not asking too much, could you give me a sign?
Let me know if this is a wise and prudent thing to do.
Yes, it seems fun and fantastic and fabulous.
But am I getting in over my head?
Should I be more practical?
Maybe, should I buy a house where I actually live now?
Not a beach shack in New York?

What was I thinking? I prayed harder and louder:

Oh God, if it is not too much trouble, would you, could you? I know, I know. Poor me, single, successful girl too scared to buy a house. Boo-hoo! Sad she has not found THE one! Silly really compared to what you are probably dealing with today, but somehow this seems huge to me. Not sure I can go through with it without your blessing. Please, Lord.

With that, I opened my eyes. When I did, I could see something coming through the sand dunes. Bright, bright colors were coming my way. Oranges and pinks and reds that seemed to be floating toward me. As they came closer, I could make out that they were long scarfs that blew in the wind. I could hear bells and chimes. It was such a sight. Like nothing I had ever seen before.

Maybe that was it? Maybe I was seeing things?

Was it a mirage? You must understand it was dusk. The beach was empty except for me and my prayers.

There, right there in front of me, was a merry band of breathtaking revelers headed my way. *Okay, God*, I thought, *maybe a bit over the top. I know that you know I am a visual learner, but this is breathtaking.* Could it really be? Was God sending me a sign?

I felt stunned and overwhelmed and humbled. I could not quite make out what it was, but as they neared, I could see it was an old woman being carried out on some kind of throne, complete with a crown on her head. She was being held up by four strong strapping gentlemen. There were maybe a dozen other men and women, girls and boys, all following along and carrying flags and banners of brightly colored pink, red, and orange cloth. They were all wearing exotic headdresses of various sorts. YES, HEADDRESSES!

I know.

I know.

Crazy but true!

It was so very beautiful. It was stunning really. Especially against the backdrop of the blue ocean and sandy beaches. Then they stopped, placed the chair where the sea meets the sand, and waited.

I slowly made my way over to the festivities. I quietly asked one of the onlookers what this gathering was all about. They explained it was their ninety-year-old aunt's birthday and her favorite thing to do was watch the sunset at the beach.

It seemed that for years she felt she was too old and feeble to go to the beach. So her nephew had worked all winter carving this throne for her in his garage, so that she could celebrate her ninetieth birthday in style as she watched the sunset on her beloved beach.

I watched in pure amazement as the peace that I should buy this house and buy it now washed over me. To land in a place with all this folly and fun and beauty and artistic glory, where an outpouring of love for, dare I say, a single aunt was present and celebrated.

Well, needless to say, that was just what this Midwestern girl needed. I was a visual learner, and it seemed God took that into account when communicating with me that day. God gave me a Technicolor-perfect answer as I sat there on the sand dunes that day.

Yep, I bought that house. And yep, it gave me so much.

A gift from a good God who heard my prayer and answered in the most personal, celebratory way.

A gift that completed me in so many ways that it could only have been orchestrated by God.

I pray you, too, look in between the sand dunes of life, because if you keep an eye out, you will see that God is also sending you a splendid parade full of color and depth that will lead you right where you need to be.

For Further Reflection

When were you sent a bold sign that answered a prayer?
How did God customize the delivery of this answer just for
   you?
How was the way God conveyed His answer a gift?

Put It into Practice

Start a conversation with God when faced with a decision.
Keep in contact with God as you weigh your options. Keep
walking closely with God as you sit in the uncertainty. Then
pay attention to magnificent signs God sends your way.

ABUNDANCE

an island

*He knows us far better than we know ourselves, knows our pregnant
condition, and keeps us present before God. That's why we can be
so sure that every detail in our lives of love for God is worked into
something good.*

ROMANS 8:27–28 MSG

I failed at becoming an actress. I had a dream in life to be a
working actress, and I failed. It is not news that Hollywood is
a tough place. I was told I was not pretty enough; I was told I was
too funny and not funny enough. They were looking for a new
face for the remake of the *Father of the Bride*. After several auditions, I was told I was just a little too new.

"You had me at hello," was one of my favorite lines from the
Jerry Maguire script. I thought no one could say it better to Tom
Cruise than I. Evidently, Renée Zellweger did. I was also told I
was just a tad too overweight.

Oh, I did get a few jobs here and there. A few national com-
mercials to keep me hooked. I was diligent about attending acting class. I learned all I could about the craft and art of acting, in
between the auditions, heartbreaks, and tears.

I supported my habit through waitressing. I hated that job so
much that I spent most of the time in the kitchen, interviewing
the chefs. How did you prepare this? How long did you cook that?

Because I was so bad at waitressing, I kept getting fired, and would move to the next restaurant, and the next cuisine.

I traveled from Italian restaurants to Japanese to Chinese to Moroccan, all the while interviewing, and soaking up all that the chefs knew. You see, while I was out daily bruising my ego, God was pushing me through His self-designed culinary school.

Because I had no money, and wanted to eat and try out my new burgeoning hobby, cooking, I started hosting dinner parties for my fellow out-of-work actors, artists, and yuppies.

I would ask each of them to bring five dollars to cover my costs, and the next thing I knew, I was giving away my waitressing shifts so I could cook for my friends' office and home parties. Friends, who had attended my fetes over the years, were hiring me to cater their gatherings. I was now making a profit cooking for my past five-dollar-a-head patrons.

Katie's Foods was born.

Then, I landed a big national commercial for Saturn cars. I took that paycheck and thought, *Maybe with this money I can stop schlepping my food around the city of Los Angeles.* Maybe my car did not always have to smell like curry or whatever I'd cooked the night before. Maybe I could take this money and open a place of my own, a place where people would have to come to me to eat my food. I joined forces with a super-talented friend of mine, Sarah Essex, and that's when my store Goat was born.

Goat was a funky place. It had a little café in the back with a coffee bar and a soup of the day. In front we sold all of our flea market finds and homemade bubble baths and salts.

We would dress up frames and pillows and sell them along with salads and sandwiches. Goat became a hangout for many of my talented friends. I watched Noah Wyle get *ER* while sitting at my counter. Mariska Hargitay landed role after role and spent some of her hard-earned money at Goat. Julianna Margulies bought many a holiday gift right there at our Goat.

I realized this was the role for me. Goat was my future, not acting. It was time to expand. I was also feeling a bit homesick, so off I went to create my second store on Mackinac Island, Michigan, or so I thought.

God's how-to took me elsewhere. On the second day of setting up the store, a man who ran the Mackinaw City Chamber of Commerce came in with a piece of paper and said that Lifetime Television just called and they were looking for the next Martha Stewart. He had told them about me, and they gave him their number for me to call.

"You tell my sisters that is not funny," I said. I mean, come on! I had been in LA for ten years, and they called Mackinac Island?

But it was no joke.

It seemed Martha Stewart was leaving Lifetime and going to CBS, and Lifetime was conducting a nationwide search for a replacement. They just happened to call Mackinac, because they thought there were a lot of artistic people living there.

Well, one thing led to another. I auditioned. I interviewed. I got the job.

Twenty years, 400 episodes, five books, a product line, a national syndicated column, and countless endorsement deals later, Katie Brown Inc. is still going.

I failed at becoming an actress so that I could become an earthly lifestyle expert. A role more fun than I could have ever imagined. A role I never could have dreamed of or played without God's formidable instruction and well-timed heavenly intervention.

For Further Reflection

How have surprising transitions transformed your life?

How has God led you through those transitions?

What were the gifts that were waiting for you when you landed?

Put It into Practice

Look back and connect the dots that have led you to your best life. Realize how the entire time God was working to deliver you to a prosperous place where you could receive all your glory and then shine with a blessed light, which will illuminate God's way.

a design giant

It was you who set all the boundaries of the earth; you made both summer and winter.

PSALM 74:17 NIV

I am a workaholic. I do not think this is a bad thing, because I really, really love what I do. It is hard for me to know sometimes when work ends and I begin. How do you separate what you do from how you work? How do you separate from how you live when what you do is to contemplate and to try to improve how to live, at home or in your life?

How do you separate things...
When the two things are...
When the two are really the same thing?

I get to work at the way I live. Well, hopefully you see my point. It is a fuzzy, hazy, gray line that is always moving. Because of this, I sometimes become exhausted before I even know it.

At this particular juncture of my life, about ten years into my career, I was worn out, used up, and had little to no creative juices left in my cabinet. I needed a break from it all. So, I took myself to Paris for a month. No, I did not speak French, nor did I know anything about Paris, nor was I one who jetted off to foreign countries. It just seemed like I would be surrounded by beauty there. I thought I could be by myself and wander the streets and get lost. I had a friend who had a friend who knew about an apartment for rent over there. So, off I sent myself.

The apartment was up a winding staircase. It was not expensive, nor was it large. It was a perfect hideout from my life of figuring out life.

As the days passed, like most workaholics, I was feeling just a bit on edge. Was the world going on without me? Didn't I need to be home and taking care of business? I was feeling so relaxed, yet I was being nudged by something deep down inside that wanted me to get moving and get back to work.

I was taking in all the beauty in one minute then the next I thought I had no business taking a "holiday" in Paris, of all places!

I was beginning to feel a slow chilled hum take over my body that was exactly what I needed. No sooner had that feeling emerged when . . . I felt like I had indulged myself long enough.

Time to get back to reality. My style game seemed to be improving with each new scarf I wrapped around my neck. And it was just so fun.

Wait a minute. I am from the Midwest and my work ethic runs deep. Therefore, I had no business taking a break from my business. My internal battle was fierce.

Did I mention I was taking, or shall I say, crashing a figure drawing course?

My sketches were really beginning to loosen up. I was finding a new direction, as I compared them to the others I saw. I was making progress.

The calls to and from my office were less and less frequent. I wondered if by unplugging I had cut myself off . . . therefore out?

I convinced one of my best friends, Sarah, who was also traveling in France, to come and spend the day and evening with me.

When she saw me, she said, "You are glowing." We walked mostly in silence along the streets, taking in the sights and sounds.

"What have you been up to?" she asked. "You seem so radiant."

We discussed everything we both had been doing as only good friends can.

Sarah said, "I gotta say it again. I feel like your light is ON."

We finished dinner and strolled out into the street. It seemed a man had followed us out of the restaurant and was trying to catch up to us. He finally did, grabbed my arm, and said something to me in French. When I looked bewildered, he quickly switched to English.

The three of us chatted a bit. He then looked me in the eye, gave me his card, and said, "Please call me tomorrow at the office so we can continue our conversation." Was he trying to pick me up? Maybe? There was something familiar about him.

He seemed very French to me with ruffled hair, big lips, and a battered leather jacket and jeans. As he sauntered away, Sarah said to me, "Do you know who that is?"

"No," I said.

"That was Philippe Starck," she informed me.

"What? It was?" I said in disbelief.

"I told you. You had your light on," she chirped.

Philippe Starck was one of my design heroes. I was not familiar with his face, but I certainly was familiar with his work. He was and is a design giant. His free-form career path was one I so admired. There were not many categories in the field of professional creativity he had not conquered.

As instructed, I dialed him up the next day. The answering

machine clicked on and a female voice spouted something in French. She then followed up with what I assumed was the same message in English. The message went something like this: "You have reached the offices of Philippe Starck. Please leave a message at the beep, but understand that we will not be responding to you until after the midday hour. The morning time is our time to daydream and think and be creative. *Bon jour.*"

Philippe Starck never returned my phone call. He did not need to. I got the message. It took an international design guru to deliver to me both in French and in English the point of my entire month spent in Paris. The message that you have to have boundaries.

I had to have boundaries. God turned my light on so that I could feel the glow and receive the word and the permission I had been looking for: the knowledge that it was okay to turn away for just a bit.

God sent the perfect messenger to assure me that there is nothing indulgent about taking time to recharge, to know where you live and where your work ends.

God got my attention all right. He was determined for me to hear it loud and clear. So determined...

That he said it in two languages...

And used a delivery service...

That was top notch...

to ensure its meaning would not be lost.

For Further Reflection

How have you established boundaries between work and play?

How has God delivered events that unfolded in a way that allowed you to achieve and understand the importance of this practice?

How has your habit of separating work and play been a gift?

Put It into Practice

Spot and determine time and space where you can recharge. Understand the importance of these places and times, and know that God wants you to indulge in both work and play so that you can reach your potential in all areas of your life.

a sandy beach

So now faith, hope, and love abide, these three; but the greatest of these is love.

1 CORINTHIANS 13:13 ESV

I was watching my toddler Prentiss play solo in the sand when I heard her whisper to someone. Like I said, she was playing by herself, so I leaned in a bit to see if I had heard correctly. Yep, she was talking, all right. It appeared as though she was talking to something she held in her hand. I looked closer and realized she was holding a wet ball of sand.

"Who are you talking to?" I asked.

"My friend Alice," she replied matter-of-factly as she held up the sand ball for further proof that she was in fact in the company of her friend, Alice, someone I had never known her to talk to before.

I continued to eavesdrop as Prentiss asked Alice questions. She seemed to chuckle at her responses. Prentiss gently shaped Alice into an even rounder, bigger ball. We were on a family vacation on an island that offered several choices of beaches, miles away from our cold, hectic home base. This particular day we had rented a convertible so that we could do some beach hopping.

Prentiss continued to play with her sand ball Alice until it was time to move on to another beach. Prentiss climbed into the back of the car with her sand ball cupped in her little hands. As we drove in the convertible, the wind whipped all around us, causing some of the sand that Alice was made of to drift away. We drove faster, made tight quick turns, barreled downhill, shifted uphill. Within minutes, most of the grains of sand had drifted from the ball and floated into the island air. I watched as Prentiss casually tossed what remained of the ball over the side of the car. I felt crestfallen for her. After all, her friend Alice had just evaporated. Yet, Prentiss seemed unfazed.

When we arrived at the next beach, I watched Prentiss create yet another ball. She gripped, loved, and conversed with this ball... until it too dried up and evaporated. She created these balls of sand again and again and again. Each with the same dedication, devotion, and love.

As a mother, I have struggled with my now fourteen-year-old daughter's social interactions. You know the motherly struggle of knowing when to jump in, help out, steer her away when I see her get hurt, get bruised, get conned by someone she considers a friend. How far do you go to help your daughter make friends, organize her, and nurture her?

I was recently attending a memorial service for the father of a friend of mine, Stephen Kittenplan. It took place in a famous massive hall in New York City. It was packed. The speeches were moving. In one of the tributes, someone stated that Stephen had been a gifted friend.

A gifted friend... I want to be a gifted friend.

Friendships were not always easy for me. I did not have a lot of time for them when I was young. Between sports, school, and my family, they seemed frivolous. They seemed not exceptionally important. Perhaps this was because my parents had few friends.

They were not really typical social people. So I had no childhood images of how friendship should look or evolve.

As I have gotten older, I have grown to believe friendships are important. They enrich my life tremendously.

I need them.

I want them.

I cherish them.

Which brings me to my next thought. I can do so much better as a friend. Some of my friends call me a unicorn because they are never sure when I will show up. Some of my friends find my Waspy-ness hard to get through. Some make fun of my competitive nature.

Friendship-gifted I am not. Well, that is not quite right. I believe I am gifted at picking good ones. I am gifted at zeroing in on true blue. I am gifted at collecting people who are just right for me. Come to think of it, I should call them my *just-right friends*.

So how do I teach my girls to jump in? How do I teach my girls how to pick and stick with their just-right friends?

When my girls come home, they tell me tales of how someone has hurt their feelings. I immediately want the names and addresses of those mean girls. When my girls have clearly been wronged, I want to lash out at those who have wronged them, and alert the authorities.

Not gifted.

Not gifted.

My first friendship journey was in middle school. Middle school can be tough years for sure, but my friend Tracey helped me get through it. We had many similarities. We had so much fun together. She was the youngest in a family with a lot of children. A few of her older siblings were in high school and college.

One night, while I was staying overnight at her house during eighth grade, her big brothers and sisters were having a party. I did not know much, but I did know that her siblings knew how to party, so I was not completely surprised.

But Tracey was not like them. She was an all-A, straight-laced athlete. I guess if I were truthful, I kind of wondered if she was going to go the way of her family. If she would walk with them on the wild side.

When we came home that night from watching our local high school football game, the party was in full bloom. It is all a bit foggy to me. I remember everyone being tall, very tall. I remember lots of drinking glasses thrown about and loud music.

Before I knew it, I could not find my Tracey. I looked everywhere for her. Finally I found her. She was hiding in the back of a closet. "PSSST," she said as I opened the door. "PSSST." There she was, tucked in between the shoes and behind the dresses.

"What are you doing in here?" I asked.

"I cannot feel my feet," she said, giggling uncontrollably. She was high, high as a kite, and loving it.

I could not reach her that night. I could not reach her very often on the nights, weeks, and months that followed. She went into that closet that night and came out forever changed.

Still Tracey.

Still smart.

Still fun.

But often high.

Often off wherever drugs and alcohol took her. Where they took her was not with me. They took her to other friends. They took her in a different direction from me.

I missed her. I missed our friendship. I was heartbroken to lose my Tracey.

Now that I am a mom, I watch my eighth-grade daughter navigate these treacherous waters with my tiger mom instincts that want to shield her from the heartbreak of broken friendships.

When I think back to that day on that sandy beach: to Prentiss's friendship with Alice, the sand ball; to the way a friendship may slip away as we speed off down the road; to the way she reinvested and regrouped through the gathering and shaping of each ball on one beach after the next, she reminded me of something fundamental. My daughter reminded me that the act of nurturing a friend over and over again is where the real satisfaction lives. Prentiss reminded me there on the beach that day that it is always worth it to reinvest and recommit to developing friendships. She reminded me that it is in these acts that we learn how to be *a gifted friend*.

Prentiss had a few balls that were packed tight enough to be wrapped in a towel and placed in her beach bag for safekeeping. Not all. But a few were formed in a way that would be just right for what she needed. As for the others? Before they left, they gifted her with a day well spent in the service of investing in companionship.

For Further Reflection

Which of your friendships are and have been worth the cost and why?

How have God's lessons in the art of friendship deepened your understanding?

How has the evolution of your friendships been a gift?

Put It into Practice

Take stock of the way friendships past and present have enriched your life. Take stock of the knowledge that friends are heaven-sent and worth the ups and the downs.

an uncle

Greater love hath no man than this, that a man lay down his life for his friends.

JOHN 15:13 KJV

I got lucky in life. I was given an angel in the form of an uncle. Uncle Meredith, to be specific. He would praise me often and seemed to value my strengths, which were a bit out of bounds for my Waspy family.

I was dramatic. He celebrated that.

I would talk back. He seemed to admire that.

I found most things funny. He would laugh with me.

I drilled down to find the simple truth of things. He always followed me in those pursuits.

In a sometimes lonely childhood, I felt I had a champion, a partner, a support, a friend, and then some. He was the uncle whom dreams were made of. He gave great Christmas presents that were wrapped in the most creative and stunning ways.

He made visits to my college, where he would take my friends and me out to restaurants that we ourselves could not afford. He would take me on fabulous shopping sprees that seemed limitless. And although all this was breathtaking, it paled in comparison to the way he made me feel seen and understood. He felt like home. Our connection was otherworldly. I was so grateful for him and for us. The way his love made this awkward middle child feel was so life changing that it cannot be overstated. The amount of confidence I drew from his affection for me is immeasurable. It has had a profound effect on who I am today.

My uncle Meredith was a single gay man who lived in San Francisco. He was a lawyer for Standard Oil and lived with his lover, Roland, who owned a shoe repair shop. I grew up with him popping in and out of my Midwestern life.

I do not remember the moment when he told me or I realized he was gay. As I matured, it was a kind of realization that slowly, uneventfully became clear. I remember one afternoon when I was a sophomore in college sitting on the beach with him, looking out at Lake Michigan, when he said, "If you ever want to ask me anything, anything, you can." I knew what he was talking about, but I did not feel like it needed to be discussed. He loved who he loved, and I loved him.

It was the early eighties and the AIDS epidemic was coming into focus. Not long after my college graduation, I was told that Uncle Meredith's lover of twenty-five years had been diagnosed with the disease. My uncle was a wreck. He struggled with caring for Roland and still continuing to work in a place where he had to keep his lifestyle close to the vest. He faced a bit of a battle to gain the clearance he needed to be present in the hospital and to be part of the choreography of his lover's treatment. It broke his heart that he could not be by his side every day, all day.

Well, he might not have been able to, but I was. I had a gap of about two weeks between graduating from college and reporting for work in New York City. My parents were hesitant for me to go to San Francisco, to say the least. The world was still searching for clarity about how people contracted AIDS. Many thought it was contagious through touching, breathing, and sharing bodily fluids. It was a scary time. My parents wanted to make sure I was protected. I wanted to be sure I was protected. But off I flew to the West Coast.

I did not have much experience with sickness. I was blessed with good health, as were most of my family and friends. I hoped I would be up for the task of sitting by Roland's bedside while my uncle worked.

I had not spent much time with Roland because Meredith always came alone to our house. With the exception of a weekend when my mother and I took the train to his city on the Pacific. Back then, I am not sure I knew who Roland was to my uncle, but like I said, as time wore on, I matured and it slowly all made perfect sense to me.

Now I was old enough to be the one to hold my Meredith up when he needed me. I knew I was taking a stand of devotion at a place and time that some might have found reckless, even foolish. But that didn't matter to me. Love did.

Roland was always a thin fella. When I arrived at his bedside, it still struck me that he was so very tiny and frail yet, as always, handsome as all get-out. It is all a bit of a blur. I do not even know how many hours or how many days I sat there. I do distinctly remember the thought that, as time passed, he seemed to be sinking into his bed. It was as if the man I recognized was rapidly disappearing right before my eyes. I am not sure I was very effective at adding much, but I was there. I showed up with all my youth and inexperience. I knew that Meredith knew I was there for him. I knew that Meredith knew I was historically about his lifestyle. But I hoped my presence also showed him that my naïveté was full of a love that knew no bounds and carried with it no judgment.

It dawned on me that this is the way God loves us. God's love knows no bounds. It's the way we need to love God back. We need to jump in. We need to show up. No matter how controversial the situation or the timing might be. No matter how much it might cost us. Our relationship with God cannot be one way. It needs to be a relationship. A give and take. And the give part? The when-we-are-needed part? We must rise, stand tall, stand with God. We must jump through and over to wherever our dedication leads us and needs us. We need to go out on a limb if need be. Mark Twain said that is where the fruit is.

My uncle's lover's illness was the first time I could jump in and take part. It was the first time I could show him that I loved him with all I had. That I loved him unconditionally, through rough waters, no matter what the circumstance.

My uncle loves me. I love my uncle.

My God loves me. I love my God.

In both relationships I must give deep and far to get to the fruit.

For Further Reflection

When did you step out in love despite the trouble, the danger or the cost?

When have you stepped out for God despite the trouble, the danger, or the cost?

How has the act of showing up for the relationships in your life been a gift?

Put It into Practice

Sacrifice for someone you love so that you can reap the benefits of giving as well as receiving. Sacrifice in your relationship with God in order to have a true relationship that will make your experience so much richer.

a flower

The Lord God took the man and put him in the garden of Eden to work it and keep it.

GENESIS 2:15 ESV

I love that moment when I first walk outside after a snowstorm and all seems peaceful. You know that moment, when the air feels like spearmint and it is bone silent. The only sound is your feet crunching into the drifts below you. It almost echoes as you march forward. In the dawn of the newly fallen blanket of peace, there is some kind of wonderful harmony that you and Mother Nature are playing—a perfectly placed footstep into the perfectly toned notes of the snow and ice breaking. You play with the sound while plowing through it, accompanied by the brushing notes of the billowing tree branches caught in the tangle of dripping snow and ice as you slide by them. This causes a fluttering reaction of *drip-dropping* flakes that accentuate the duet you and Mother Nature are singing.

This interaction, and more of the like, are the moments I feel that God is right there with me, shadowing my every move. It is not dramatic. I am not in the heat of a crisis. I am not at a crossroads. I am simply gob-stopped by the majesty of the mother, Mother Nature, that is.

The great outdoors to me is God's craft room. God's art gallery open to the public twenty-four/seven. But like any great children's art museum, when it is viewed and understood to be interactive, well, in the words of Dr. Seuss, "Oh, the places you'll go!"

In my work, I always refer to nature as my muse—my greatest source of inspiration for projects, for design, for layouts, for colors, for combinations. When I combine my sense of style with her *objets d'art*, oh, the places we go!

One childhood spring, Mother Nature took my mom on a ride that spotlights the kind of partnership I am expressing perfectly. I grew up in Northern Michigan, and gardening in that region is not for the faint of heart. However, my mother would not be deterred. She experimented, tried, studied, dug, and planted any and all sorts of flowers and plants. My mom was determined to prove she would and could create a picture-perfect landscape as the backdrop for our home.

We had begonias, tulips, impatiens, lilies of the valley, gladiolus, and her all-time favorite, lilacs. You name it, she tried to make it thrive. But it was one accidental spring seedling that left an everlasting impression on her, on me, and on anyone else who did and still does pass by the house.

In an attempt to save money one year, my mother ordered her bulbs from a discount mail order catalog. As a gift with the purchase, she received a few packages of bluebell seeds.

What joy! She was thrilled. She plotted. She planned. She began to dig small trenches along both edges of the sidewalk leading to our front door. As she gazed at the photo on the front of the package, she imagined what a grand impression these tall blooming blue flowers would be as one walked up to our welcoming home.

Well, as fate would have it, these blue gems were the first glimpse of color for the spring season. The rub was that they were tiny, small, mini blue flower heads. It was ground cover really. Not at all the tall, grand colonnade she had imagined from the depiction on the package photo. In fact, it was quite the opposite. The bluebells seemed to be held captive in those manmade trenches along our walk. Oh, the disappointment, the embarrassment, and the frustration due to those bright blue duds.

With the next spring just around the corner, my mom had a new and improved garden in the works. The disastrous blue babes were barely a memory. As early spring arrived, we waited for our newly planted bulbs to blossom. Much to our surprise, the first dash of color to arrive? The ill-fated bluebells. Only this time, they were not confined to the deep ditches she had created for them the previous year. This year they had spread across the entire front yard. They created a delicate blue dust scattered among the early spring grass that was just struggling to turn green.

What a sight! Year after year after year after year those bluebells announced the beginning of spring as they multiplied and cast a magnificent blue shimmer across the front lawn. People would slow down as they passed by just to gaze a bit longer at the blue blaze of early spring. It was a welcome sight after all the long gray winter days. Mother Nature had joined forces with my mother to captivate those who saw our house come to life spring after spring.

Mother Nature wrote a song that, when my mom sang along, sounded more glorious than my earthly mother could have ever imagined. God took notes and played a haunting harmony far more smashing than my mom could have ever dreamed up.

The legacy of their duet lives on. Although we no longer live in that home, an old friend recently told us that the bluebells spread to the backyard.

Those bluebells planted by my mother and spread by the hand of God created yet another blue oasis for all to enjoy.

When we paint on GOD's canvas, when we collaborate with the world's greatest living artist, be prepared to be transported to a land full of the greatest beauty and color and music of all time.

For Further Reflection

When was the last time you created a project based in nature?
How did your interaction with Mother Nature turn into something even more wonderful than you imagined?
How was God's elevation of your hopes and dreams a gift?

Put It into Practice

Collaborate and commune with Mother Nature. Then listen, watch, and wait for God to raise the view and the beauty above your greatest expectations.

a tree

For everything there is a season, and a time for every matter under heaven: a time to be born, and a time to die; a time to plant, and a time to pluck up what is planted; a time to kill, and a time to heal; a time to break down, and a time to build up; a time to weep, and a time to laugh; a time to mourn, and a time to dance; a time to cast away stones, and a time to gather stones together; a time to embrace, and a time to refrain from embracing.

ECCLESIASTES 3:1–5 ESV

*T*he *Giving Tree*, by Shel Silverstein, is a book that describes a relationship between a tree and a boy. The tree gives to the boy at every stage of his life. As a child, he swings from the tree's branches when he wants to play. When the boy gets hungry, the tree gives him apples. When he is cold, the tree gives him wood to start a fire. The tree allows him to rest upon him when he is tired, and then lets him float away in its trunk when he needs to leave.

I think I relate to this story because I believe it's the way I relate to my homes, my houses, my four walls. I hope the walls I live in get a lot from me as I tend to their design and repair needs, but I often feel like my homes give me more than they get. Granted, I have an unusually thoughtful and intimate relationship with my homes. Perhaps this is because of what I do for a living. To be clear, my entire adult life has been about all things home. A house and what it takes to turn that house into a home is my life's work and my passion, both professionally and personally. To me this work is deeper than just furniture arranging, choosing wall colors, party menus, or gift wrap. To me, my work is, was, and always will be about how to turn that house into a safe haven where people can create important traditions, confidences, intimacies, and securities. My work is to highlight the important role that a home can play in so many different ways in the development of a family's lifestyle. My houses and I have moved together through this life hand in hand. Please indulge me as I make my case...

The first home I ever bought was really just two old barns and a butcher shop that came together to form an eclectic house on Butter Lane. The house was all mine. It came to me at a time in my life when I felt adrift. I was single in my late thirties and this house—it became my anchor. It was a place for me to dock during my career-driven days. I made it mine with each wall I painted and sink I installed. We became close. It acted as a beacon in my single life, a bright, bold banquet hall, for me and my posse to let the good times roll.

Next, it became my backdrop for a love story with a man who became my husband. Within months, it was time for me to transform my guest bedroom into a nursery for my firstborn baby.

Now we were four and we needed more.

When we sold it, it seemed my two old barns and a butcher shop on Butter Lane had more than tripled in value. So, that house sent me off with a richer fanfare than I could ever have imagined. The gold it provided me with delivered me into the arms of a tall townhouse in the heart of the city.

The townhouse was tops. Soon, the townhouse and I also became close. It was more mature like myself and my family. To accentuate that, I dosed it with distinguished lights, willful wall-paper, and plush carpets. My family flourished in that four-story steely lady. It was our protector from a forceful city.

Soon my family needed to move on and out to the country. The tall townhouse that I had bought with my two old barns and a butcher shop had also more than tripled in value, so it sent me off again with a richer fanfare than we could have ever imagined. The gold it provided us with delivered us into a big old "Betty" of a rambling antique house, from where I wrote this book.

The boy had a giving tree and I had a giving home. They both tell a story of selfless love through life's seasons.

At this point in my life and my career, I am doing what is called a pivot. I am adapting my professional life that to-date has focused only on all things that make up a family home. Now I'm including a focus on my previously very personally held and private beliefs about and relationship with God. This relationship includes a different kind of home. It includes my relationship with my church home, a home that I believe has also given more to me than I have to it.

My church home, like my personal home, has walked hand in hand with me through the seasons of my life. It, too, has been my giving tree when I have been in need at various stages of my growth.

Again allow me to explain.

When I was a child, I suffered under the roof of what I felt was an overly punishing dad. The church delivered to me a Father who comforted me with a kind, gentle love.

When I struggled with being a less-than-satisfactory student at my school desk, the church gave me a Sunday school desk where I could shine.

When I needed to go deep with my fiancé, my church gave me a formal forum in its parlor to discuss and discover how we might tackle future foundational issues as we built a life together.

When I needed a place that would plant the seeds of a moral compass in my beautiful daughters, my church gave me vacation Bible school, youth choir, weekly family dinner, confirmation classes, and an old-fashioned Sunday school.

A tree is more than a collection of branches.

A home is more than a series of rooms.

A church is more than a religious sanctuary.

It is a caring collection of four walls. And if you go, if you give, if you plant your roots in a church, much like you do in a family home, it will love you and provide for you in unconditional ways. So, no matter what room in life you are living in, no matter what season you are weathering, God's church trunk will lift you up. God's church branches will support you through the many stages of an abundant well-lived life.

For Further Reflection

Where does your soul go for shelter? In what place or space have you experienced a recurring bond and nurturing love throughout the years?

Did you feel the embrace of God when you experienced the generous security in that place?

How has this space or place been a continued gift?

Put It into Practice

Consider the church's unique ability to meet you exactly where you're at. If you haven't already, find a church home that can nurture and encourage you no matter what season of life you're in.

HOPE

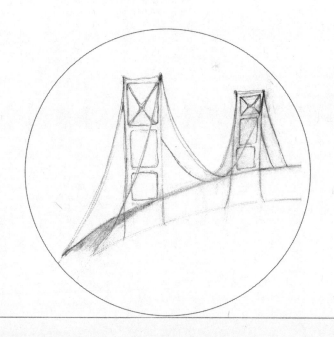

a cell phone

But those who hope in the LORD will renew their strength. They will soar on wings like eagles; they will run and not grow weary, they will walk and not be faint.

ISAIAH 40:31 NIV

I had never spoken out publicly about my faith until maybe ten or so years ago when my mother asked me to. She said she would like it if I would agree to be a breakout speaker at a Christian women's retreat that she had started with some friends of hers. That first retreat, I believe, was a luncheon with about twenty women. At the point that she asked me to participate, it was up to six two-day, back-to-back retreats per year with about a thousand women at each retreat at the Grand Hotel on Mackinac Island, Michigan.

You want me to talk about my faith? Seemed kind of private to me. It seemed to me that talking about my faith to an audience was kind of above my pay grade. Furthermore, talking about my faith to others seemed kind of like bragging that my Christian habits were worthy of that kind of evangelism. And, wow, I was not sure that was the case. However, she is my mother, and as they say, *She knows best.* So there I was at the retreat blabbing away.

The speech I gave was really the beginning of this book.

I told many of the same stories that are written in many of these pages.

Stories that, as I prepared my speech that day, did seem to have a certain rhyme and reason...

A real pattern, if you will...
  Of the strength of GOD...
    To guide you and send you messages...
      To talk to you and walk with you.

Stories that almost all ended in a way that made sense out of the situations I would find myself in. When I looked at them in that space where God and my life intersected, they were my divine stories, divine stories from my heart and soul.

Well, that day, I ended my talk with the beginning of yet another challenging story I found myself in. Here is the way I ended that speech ten years ago on that day:

> Four years of in vitro fertilization, several miscarriages, and three failed, horrific adoption attempts. I'm not sure where this immense pain is going to leave me. I am not sure what to do with the powerful jealousy that fills me when I see a pregnant woman and her swollen belly, and I think, Why not me? I don't know what to do with the years of memories of my husband shooting me up with hormones, thinking, surely this time it's going to work, only to once again hear the painful, slow, patient tone of my doctor's nurse on the other end of the phone, saying one more time, "We are sorry for your loss." But I know, as I look toward and open up to my Life-style Guru, God above, He will show me the beauty in this despair.

After I delivered these last words of my final speech, I grabbed my phone and walked off the stage. Please note, over those four days of three back-to-back, twenty-four-hour retreats, I had to deliver this speech six times, each time to a crowd of three-hundred-plus women. Did I mention I had never talked about my faith publicly before this?

As I walked out into the hallway and glanced at my phone, I saw I had a missed message from our adoption lawyer. I debated whether or not to call him back because my husband and I had already decided not to continue our search. It was just too heart-breaking. Prentiss, William, and I had decided we were all the family we would be. And that would be just fine.

But I did call that lawyer back. "We have an adoption match for you and I feel really good about this one," he said.

I held my breath for a minute, cried a bit, said a prayer, then dialed up the baby's birth mother, right there in the lobby of that hotel...minutes after finishing my first public faith talk.

One month later we brought Meredith, our newly adopted baby, *home*.

I know.

I know.

Some may say this is just a coincidence.

Maybe?

I know.

I know.

Some may say, "Oh, God keeps score like that and the winning prize is a baby?"

Come on.

I know.

I know.

Seems too obvious.

Seems, I don't know, maybe just too simple?

The thing is, you have to know that I did not know from that message from my lawyer that day that this would be the baby that would be ours. I did not know from that message from my lawyer that day that it would lead to our Meredith. You have to know that it was not until I began to write this story for this book that I even did the math that led me to the conclusion that I started on the path toward Meredith that day, minutes after reading those words.

You see, as I walked through the difficult doors of trying to witness about my faith, filled with all my self-doubt and loathing...

You see, as I walked through the difficult doors of infertility, with all my inner sorrow and grieving, my faith was bright that day...

It was bright enough for me to have the faith to lean in once again and surrender to a process where I had little to no control. I had overcome my insecurities long enough to speak my truth about my relationship with God. I had to overcome my grief long enough to be open to the possibility of the dream of finding a sibling for my Prentiss.

God lit up my cell phone and matched my light with His love, His grace, and one of the biggest blessings of my family's life... OUR MEREDITH.

So sing! Sing loud and proud. Do your own spiritual math. Take the time to draw your own spiritual map. Sew your own religious patterns together.

When you do...

the results,

the music,

the chorus,

the collage,

will brighten your way.

For Further Reflection

When have you shared about your faith?

When have you taken stock in your faith long enough to uncover how your own personal walk with God has led you to where and who you are today?

How has sharing about your faith in God been a gift?

Put It into Practice

Do not be afraid to shine a light on your faith, because when you do, a shift will happen.

circles and squares

But Jesus called the children to him and said, "Let the little children come to me, and do not hinder them, for the kingdom of God belongs to such as these."

LUKE 18:16 NIV

I am not going to say I'm immature in my faith. I am not going to say I am underdeveloped in my faith. But I am not a theologian or a minister. I am not even sure I am a devoted enough Christian to be able to have the nerve to write this book.

My relationship with God goes something like this: I talk to God like I talk to a girlfriend. I wake with: "Hi there, it's me, Katie. I love You. Be with me if You got the time today." We have many a conversation throughout the day.

I see God.

I feel God.

I chat with God.

It's not formal; it's usually fun and playful. Unless I am in pain and need a shoulder to lean on. I rarely ask Him for specifics. It seems to me that that would be presumptuous. I just kind of turn myself over to God.

To me, every sunrise is a new opportunity to walk a bit closer to God. When I focus on God, it feels like I am free falling. Like I am trying to fly where God's winds lead me. As I soar through the twists and turns and watch the world, my world unfolds from a vantage point that is, to quote one of my favorite sayings, "in the world but not of the world." A vantage point that is not in the church but is of the church.

My relationship with the Holy feels youthful. It feels joyous and freeing and fun. I rarely take a knee but I always lower my head and my gaze when talking to God. Sometimes I am seeking and God seems to be hiding, or at times I am hiding and God is seeking.

I rarely feel much older than twelve when we discuss our daily goings-on. In many ways, God is my best friend, my number one. God is as breathtaking to me as when I look out on fresh snow, smooth and fresh and glistening and silent and not yet touched by anything on earth.

If I had to simply sum it up, my relationship with God feels childlike.

There was an experience in my life I remember so clearly, where I believe God was telling me that a childlike perspective is nothing to be ashamed of. It was the first day of Professor Singer's Painting 101 class my freshman year at Cornell University.

I walked into the class and there in the center of the room was a naked lady standing on a pedestal. There were a series of chairs and easels scattered about. Some students had already set up their large pad of paper and were busily sketching. I had never done real-life drawing before. I am embarrassed to admit, I was more than a little bit stunned to be confronted with such blatant naked-ness, but so it went with my newfound major. This would be the first of many figures I was tasked to draw in all their glory.

I put pencil to paper and began. The room was silent, the only sound the movement of mark to paper. I found I could not really move. I could not really make a stroke. I was panicked. I looked around and everyone seemed so focused, so determined to get it right. They did not seem timid or scared, but rather confident and eager. I could tell that most, if not all, of them had participated in this kind of exercise many times before. I was frozen as I watched my fellow pupils draw this lovely lady perfectly. Their perspective was flawless. Their shading made the figure seem to come alive.

Finally, I snapped out of it and got busy. As my drawing unfolded in front of me, I seemed to draw only shapes. For example, I drew a triangle for a breast and a square for a shoulder. The more I tried to make the model look more lifelike, the more her figure morphed into a collection of various shapes.

Before I knew it, the time was up. The model threw on her clothes and made her way out of the classroom. We were now to take these sketches and turn them into a painting.

Wait!
What?
A painting?
Out of my shapes?
God, help please.

Professor Singer explained that at the end of the week we would do a class critique on our pieces. *Save me,* I thought.

The others got on with it. Their oil paintings were colorful and bold and full of depth and accuracy. For some reason, I did not see my lady as colorful, but rather as a series of shades that included only whites, grays, and blacks. *Which one of these is not like the other?* I thought to myself. *Ahhhh...* that would be mine! Mine looked so juvenile.

The day arrived when all paintings were on display. At the front of the class, the professor called us up one by one to stand side by side with our painting and explain our viewpoint and answer questions.

My painting stood out like a sore thumb. It looked like a paint-by-number piece of art. A paint-by-number kit painting that had a limited palette, because they had used up all the vivid colors. The discussions were full of back-and-forth and deep explanations of how each student achieved their goals throughout the paintings.

My turn. I stood up there next to my painting just as tall as I could, knowing how ridiculous my infantile piece looked. The room was silent for what seemed like too long, when my very tall professor, who had long flowing curly gray hair, stood up and came close to my painting. He took his time as he looked it up and down. He turned to me, then he turned to the class and said, "What Katie has achieved is something you all should strive for. She has accomplished what every artist hopes for." He then quoted Picasso, " 'Every child is an artist. The problem is how to remain one when we grow up.'

"All of you must be careful to remain true to your childlike perceptions. So that you can create without judgment, because that is where you will hook into your real artistry."

WOW! Perhaps a far too generous and sympathetic characterization of my abilities, but I took it!

While writing this book, I had to lean on that moment often. Because, you see, my understanding and relationship with God, Jesus, and the Holy Ghost is as inexperienced as I was in that class so many years ago. It is just as pure as my underdeveloped combination of colorless shapes. I stood up there in the front of that class that day with a deep satisfaction that I knew exactly what Professor Singer was talking about. I knew that no matter how hard I tried, I would never see or be able to produce anything like my extremely talented fellow students had seen and created.

I stood up there even taller in that moment, knowing that my perceptions were quite enough to land me right where I was.

I stand here today with this group of simple stories that I believe hold as deep a meaning as my circles and squares did that day.

I stand here today with my group of stories with all their theological naïveté, hoping that my hard-earned childlike vantage point of faith will be enough to help you on your walk as much as it has helped me on my walk.

I stand here today begging you to meet God with the wonder and amazement and simplicity of a child as you interpret your own moments experienced in that *space between*, where all God's children are welcome.

For Further Reflection

How do you see, trust, and honor your youthful perspective?

How has God reassured you that you are enough when you stand and view a situation and the world through your seemingly naïve vantage point?

What gifts are in plain view when you see through childlike eyes what would otherwise go unnoticed?

Put It into Practice

Meet God with the wonder and curiosity of a child and discover the worth of your perspective and talent.

a billboard

When you pass through the waters, I will be with you; and when you pass through the rivers, they will not sweep over you. When you walk through the fire, you will not be burned; the flames will not set you ablaze.

ISAIAH 43:2 NIV

I was on a natural high. I could not believe my fate. I was in the back of a cab driving through the streets of New York, and I had just sold my first cookbook. Let me say that again: I had just sold my first cookbook. It was all just too exciting.

I was on a professional roll. I had a hit TV show. I had done some high-profile endorsements. I had done numerous national talk shows demonstrating cooking and crafting projects. My high-powered agents said the next step was a book!

I must admit that it terrified me to write a book.

This book deal that we had just secured was the culmination of my walking in and out of various publishers' offices and laying out the look, the feel, and the content of my proposed book. The whole while, I was hoping that no one would see my knees shaking under the conference table.

As I was doing these dog and pony shows, my agents and I had gone on a fishing expedition, and I caught one. A real publisher who wanted to publish a real book written by ME! Me, who is someone, who most of the time, still turns her letters around and spells more phonetically than correctly.

It was all so thrilling. I was beside myself. Really, I was right there in the backseat of the cab, but I felt like I was sitting right there next to myself saying, *You? Who do you think you are?* That's right, it did not take long for me to go from cloud nine to disbelief to complete and utter self-doubt. All the red flags and warning lights that I had managed to keep at bay during the pitching process were now all systems go! I felt paralyzed with uncertainty.

ME? Write a book?

Oh, what have I done?

ME? Write a book?

What a fraud I am.

How am I going to pull this off?

The fact that I can't spell is the least of it.

How does one write a book?

How many recipes?

How many pictures?

How many tabletops?

How many words?

How many sentences?

How do I write a book?

I was panicked. I felt really small in the back of that cab. It did not help that we were nearing Times Square with all the bright lights and signs and traffic that seemed larger than life. With my fear-filled eyes, I looked up and out the window. Right *there* in BIG BOLD black and white letters, three words were stretched across a billboard smack dab in the center of the square: JUST DO IT!

JUST DO IT. You might remember the Nike ad campaign that started not long before I had found myself in the back of this cab. Sure . . . I had heard this phrase before and I've heard it many times since. But as is the case with many clichés when we hear them: In the right place at the right time, it hits us in a whole new way. Sometimes in an otherworldly way or, as I like to think of it, in a Godly way.

I really needed THAT particular message right then and there. I chuckled as I looked out that cab window. I took a deep breath and realized I just had to put one foot in front of the other just like the sign from On High said.

Sometimes in life we do not need a checklist of all the reasons not to move, nor do we need a checklist of all the reasons to move.

Sometimes a cliché, those few words, can seem so mighty . . . so right on, so obvious that it almost seems silly. I hear you. You're saying, "Well, yeah sure, but come on . . . life is not that simple. JUST DO IT? Really?"

REALLY! That sign was confirming that I needed to just do it. Just put one foot in front of the other.

God was spelling out for me how to move forward.

God was telling me, *You got this.*

God was reassuring me that I had what it takes.

God was telling me to trust . . . to have faith.

Not necessarily in myself, because as I already told you, at that moment my self-esteem did not exist, but I was listening to something bigger than I. I believed that something even bigger than that sign and even bigger than Times Square would lift me up. God was telling me, in such a simple, obvious way, that little, flawed me did not need to have all the answers or all the know-how. God was telling me to JUST DO IT, and something bigger than I would deliver the what, the where, and the how to fulfill my goal of being a published author.

When this book is published, it will be my sixth book. Furthermore, as I write this book, I am looking at a photo on my desk of a billboard featuring me in an advertisement for one of my television shows . . . in the middle of Times Square!

"But Jesus looked at them and said, 'With man this is impossible, but with God all things are possible'" (Matthew 19:26 ESV).

Just do it.

Do not judge it.

Just do it.

Let it roll out as it will.

Just do it.

Just bring your best. God *will* take care of the rest.

For Further Reflection

When have you jumped into challenges of life despite feeling inadequate?

How did your trust in God help you take the plunge?

How did diving into the deep end deliver gifts that were beyond your biggest dreams?

Put It into Practice

Jump into a life that will push your limits while you hold tight to God's hand. Trust that, with God, you have all that you will need to swim in all sorts of waters.

a diving board

Train up a child in the way he should go; even when he is old he will not depart from it.

PROVERBS 22:6 ESV

In 1972, Micki King won a gold medal at the Munich Olympics. Micki was ten when she started diving at her local YMCA. I was nine, almost ten years old. I was from Petoskey, Michigan. She was from Pontiac, Michigan. We were both Michiganders! I was mesmerized.

She was tall and blond with a big wide smile. To me, she seemed to own the world. She was so charismatic and her dives were awe-inspiring. When I watched the Olympic Medal Ceremony, it was forever cemented in my brain. I wanted to be just like her.

"Dad," I said, "I want to be an Olympic diver."

Without missing a beat, his response was, "You should be." My diving career was launched... no matter that we had no pool in my town.

I found myself in a situation similar to one Micki had also been in early in her career. When Micki arrived at the University of Michigan, women could not compete in varsity athletics. The University of Michigan's Coach Kimball famously pushed back: "I do not coach women or men; I coach people."

Later in life, I found a quote from Micki describing how she and her coach found a way to make it work: "We used the women's pool at the CCRB. What was ironic was that the men were allowed to come in and use the women's pool, but the women couldn't even come into the men's pool. Coach Kimball would sneak us through the back doors because the front door was right in front of the office of the administrators. We used the spectator bathroom and used washcloths and the public sink as a shower. We thought we were lucky."

I practiced my three-point victory wave on the swim raft on Lake Michigan. I practiced my flips and dives in the pools of hotels we were lucky enough to check into. My dad cheered me on. I imagined he, like me, was daydreaming about what it would be like when I took the Olympic diving podium. I felt lucky.

Micki had a twenty-six-year career in the Air Force. She was the first woman to hold a faculty position at a U.S. military academy, where she was a physical education instructor and diving coach. She was also the only female coach in any sport to coach a male athlete to a NCAA championship.

It never occurred to me that competing as a diver in the Olympics would be impossible for me due to the fact that, *allow me to say it again*, we had NO pool and NO diving board available to us anywhere in our town. Not to mention there wasn't a coach or team. You get the drift. But my dad did not falter. While we were at the pool in French Lick, Indiana, where the hotel where we were staying had not one but two diving boards, he taught me how to dive with as little a splash as possible. An essential skill to have if you want to medal in the Olympics.

While serving in the Air Force, Micki sat on a committee that led the way for admitting women into U.S. military academies. Micki's daughter graduated from the Air Force Academy in 2004.

On her graduation day, she presented her mother with the class ring, saying, "If anyone deserves it, my mother does."

No, I never did become an Olympic diver or an Olympian of any sort. But I did become a champion skier. Success in that sport was way more realistic, growing up in the winter wonderland that is Northern Michigan. I skied well enough to earn a varsity letter from Cornell University, which I promptly presented to my father.

Yes, Micki was my hero. And what a fine hero she was. It seemed she, too, had a hero in her coach, just like I had a hero in my father. Both saw no limits to what we could accomplish, no matter the barriers. The lesson that I could do and be anything was illustrated to me during those Olympics at age nine when my father barely blinked at my Olympic diving dreams, and went on to support them.

The truth is, I also had an advantage. I had a leg up and a head start in the ability to embrace this can-do attitude. You see, this message was drilled into me time and time again during my Sunday school classes. In those classes:

I learned about tiny David defeating Goliath.

I listened to the story of how the humble Moses parted the Red Sea.

I heard about young Jeremiah, who preached with wisdom far beyond his years.

I admired Gideon, who led an army of three hundred farmers to defeat over one hundred thousand seasoned soldiers.

I was blessed by being introduced early and often in my church home to the idea of the unlimited possibilities God affords His children.

When you grow up in the church, you grow up with Bible

stories that highlight the limitlessness of possibilities when God is your coach. You are encouraged to compete in life with the confidence that God is running races with you and is the architect of your plays. You are taught that God is cheering you on, no matter what the obstacles. The possibility of winning is fostered through the Bible's teachings.

So, no I did not have a diving board.

But I did have a few fathers...

one Heavenly and one right here on Earth...

who had trained me to believe

that I had everything a champion athlete could need

to cross whatever finish line I strived to reach.

For Further Reflection

What hero inspired you to take on a seemingly insurmountable goal?

When did you feel God's coaching and cheering you through the race of reaching your goal?

How was the journey of attempting to do something that seemed beyond your reach a gift?

Put It into Practice

Help yourself in finding the strength you need to achieve the unachievable, by studying the biblical heroes.

Pay it forward by reaching out to a child in your life. Champion them by helping them find their hero and the confidence they need to overcome their limitations.

an apron

Therefore take up the whole armor of God, that you may be able to
withstand in the evil day, and having done all, to stand firm.

EPHESIANS 6:13 (ESV)

The first meeting I had with Lifetime Television about the possibility of hosting a Lifestyle show was intimidating, to say the least. Days before the meeting, I spoke on the phone with an intern from Lifetime who explained that they needed a cook, a crafter, an artistic type who also knew their way around a garden for a new TV show they were producing. She asked me to send photos of parties that I had catered, homemade gifts that I had made, and flower arrangements that I had created.

WOW! Okay. Okay . . . I thought.

As she was reciting the list of photos she needed, I thought, *How can I get this gig?* My struggling twenty-something self was pretty excited. How could I make this happen? During that initial phone call, in that very moment, I thought fast. I told her a lie. I told her that I was going to be in New York City the following week. Because, just because, I thought maybe, just maybe, if I personally walked her through my photos, I would stand a better chance.

My thinking went like this: On paper, I would seem WAY too young and inexperienced. But maybe if I could get in front of them, if I could talk through my photos in front of them, then maybe, just maybe, my youth and inexperience would be over-shadowed by my enthusiasm.

She said that if I was coming to New York, she would be more than happy to meet. So, we set up a time and place to meet, and off I went. The meeting went so well that at the end of it, she asked if I would come to Lifetime headquarters the next morning to meet with more people.

I walked into a Lifetime conference room full of chic-looking women who were mostly dressed in black. They all had folders in front of them that had my name, "Katie Brown," written on the tab. My heart sank to my feet. *Oh my, this is for real*, I thought. I felt so inadequate. I would, for sure, be found out not to be even close to qualified. *Please, God, just let me walk out of here with my dignity.*

They began the interview by shooting questions at me. "What are women's design mistakes?" they asked.

"They don't trust themselves," I answered.

"What's your favorite recipe?" was the next question.

"Veggie chili," I said as I thought, *Breathe, Katie, breathe.*

"Who taught you how to cook?"

"No one," I said. And went on to explain, "My mother always told me: You love to eat, you will learn to cook."

Slow it down. Do not talk so loud, I said to myself.

"Who are your biggest influences?" they asked.

"My family," I answered. "My aunt Barb throws in a handful of sugar to just about everything. My aunt Ruth has the best cin-namon quick-bread recipe. My aunt Nan has never met a color she didn't like and designed a circular house on the shores of Lake Michigan so she could have views everywhere. My uncle Moey, who grew the reddest tomatoes you ever saw. Oh, and then there is the caramel ice-cream recipe that most of my relatives make at Christmas, and compete with each other over who has the best technique."

Okay, okay, breathe, Katie, I thought, trying to calm myself. *I am still cutting it.*

"What is the difference between West Coast style and East Coast style?" they chirped.

"Well, hmm," I said. After a bit of a pause, I said, "I can only answer you as if I were an apron. If I were an apron from the Midwest, I would be a half apron with some kind of a ruffle around the bottom decorated with a block print of some type of fruit. If I were an apron on the East Coast, I would be pinstriped, well pressed, and would tie around the neck and waist. If I were from the West Coast, you would never catch me in an apron."

I got this! I thought as I finished up my answer. *I can do this.* My twenty-something self was on FIRE!

I was so proud of my analogy, and it seemed to have worked because I got the job!

I have looked back on that day and that answer many times. However, I have found that analogy useful in only one other instance. The instance of describing and answering one other question. The question of my faith. The question of why my faith leads me to church.

My response? Again, I can only answer as if I were an apron. Because I believe churches are one of the aprons God provides. It seems to me, aprons are like churches. They are humble, practical, useful, helpful, and necessary. Like most aprons, these worldly church institutions are not perfect. They are not foolproof. But if you try a few on, you can find the one that works for you. You may need a plastic apron. You may want an apron with a joke on it. You might prefer to tie yourself up in a gingham number. God has a Holy Congregation just your style.

I know from which I speak. I have moved more than I care to admit. I move more than anyone I know. And so one of the first places I seek as I am getting familiar with my new community is a church or an "apron" that will be the right shield for me. I listen to the minister. I tune into the choir. I test the coffee hour and potluck dinner food. I go to one, two, three, four, or more local churches. I go one, two, three, four, and more times. As I try on these various places of worship, I pray for guidance. I walk through the doors as a humble servant of God who seeks the right fit in order to learn and grow.

God will meet you.

God will lead you.

God will wrap you up with the faith apron you need to get through any challenging recipe life demands you to cook.

Every place of worship is an apron of sorts. Not one is better than the other. They are just different. But if you cook or if you live a life where you are continually striving, then you will recognize the apron that can protect and aid you best. You will know which one will work for you and why.

No matter where you live:

the East,

the West,

the Midwest,

there is a church apron waiting for you.

So wrap a few around your life until you find one that fits. Then tie that one on tightly and see how it protects and comforts and gives you freedom to grow in faith, in peace, in joy, in hope, and in love.

For Further Reflection

When have you felt the support of a church or been shielded by a spiritual community?

Did you feel the presence of God's welcoming, caring, and protective love in that place of worship?

How has your participation in this community delivered the gift of a sense of belonging and well-being?

Put It into Practice

Determine what qualities you are looking for or would like to foster in your church that will help support you most. Make a list; write it down. Ask yourself what characteristics you would like to find or establish in a church community in order to arm yourself with what you need to be the most productive and spiritual you.

a bridge

"For truly, I say to you, if you have faith like a grain of mustard seed, you will say to this mountain, 'Move from here to there,' and it will move, and nothing will be impossible for you."

MATTHEW 17:20 ESV

Prentiss M. Brown is a figure who looms large over my family. He was my grandfather. He was also a U.S. congressman, a U.S. senator, and a vice-presidential nominee. He was a father of seven and grandfather of thirty-three. He introduced and headed up the Office of Price Administration during World War II. He was chairman of the board of Detroit Edison. I could go on, but you get the picture.

All these accomplishments are made even more remarkable when one realizes what a humble background he came from. Dad Brown (our name for my grandfather) grew up on the shores of Lake Michigan in a small town named St. Ignace. He was raised by his alcoholic father, James Brown, who was rumored to have married three or four times. James was a lawyer by trade who could deliver a speech like no other. Suffice it to say, he was a functioning alcoholic.

Prentiss's mother, Minnie Gagnon, who was French and, legend has it, very beautiful, lived about fifty-five miles away in a town called Charlevoix. She died when he was nine.

If you know any Michiganders, you know we hold up our hand to illustrate where we live on the map. Yep, it is convenient to be from a mitten-shaped state, and this occasion is no exception. My grandfather's hometown was in the Upper Peninsula, just on the other side of the tip of the mitt.

The story of how he landed in St. Ignace goes like this: James, my grandfather's father, followed the lumber business up to Northern Michigan, where those clients and the trade brought him to St. Ignace. Supposedly, he stopped moving because when he stood on the shores of the town on the bay, its beauty took his breath away. "This is my home," he claimed. That bay has been home to the majority of my family for four generations.

When my grandfather grew up, there was a ferry boat that connected the two peninsulas of Michigan. As a young lawyer, Prentiss had to adjudicate a case in front of the State Supreme Court of Michigan, located downstate in Lansing, the state capital.

As happened often back in the day, the ice would become so thick that the ferry got stuck. My grandfather and the other passengers had to walk across the strait in order to get to the train to Lansing. On that day and on many days before and after, Dad Brown would daydream about connecting his beloved Northern Michigan with its bottom half, thus making the Upper Peninsula less isolated.

Eventually, he went on to lead the march that built that bridge. He would often refer to it as his greatest gift, his greatest lasting legacy he was able to deliver to the people of the great state of Michigan. Today, when you travel across that bridge, you can pay the toll with a commemorative token that bears his face and the caption *The Father of the Bridge*. His father James's decisive moment to put down roots on that bay, on the tip of the Upper Peninsula, changed the trajectory of that territory due to my grandfather's daydream.

All this seems very high flying, almost mythical, or at least it does to me. However, my grandfather was anything but larger than life . . . In real life Dad Brown was a humble man who always returned home to St. Ignace.

No matter how many pictures I see of my Dad Brown with the great luminaries of his day, to me he was the witty-whiskered, tender, patient man who would drive me in his Cadillac, wearing his cardigan sweater, to the Wigwam to get Brach's pink chalky mints.

My dad said that one of Dad Brown's strengths was his ability to make things simple. He had the rare ability to boil complex issues down into simple concepts. Even his peers and political foes remarked to my dad how they admired Dad Brown's ability to convey lofty intentions in practical ways.

My grandfather was a brilliant man who had a hard-won simple touch. His mind was blessed with so much ability and smarts, yet his heart and history were rooted in the commonplace.

My dad tells a story that illustrates this part of his father's character beautifully. My father once asked him on what thinking he based his faith in God. Dad Brown answered without even blinking or seemingly thinking. He stated simply, "There is no other choice," almost as if it was so obvious that there was no need for a deep, complex explanation.

There is no other choice.

U.S. Senator Phil Hart, when giving my grandfather's eulogy, told the story of how, as a youth of seventeen, he was working his first job away from home. On the Great Lakes' steamer called *The Chippewa*, he slept in a large room filled with bunks that slept a dozen or more hard-boiled men. He wondered if he could, in that crowd, continue his habit of kneeling in prayer before bed. It was quite a struggle for the seventeen-year-old, but with fear and trembling, he did it. He knelt by his bed and prayed. As he did, there followed a very long silence. My grandfather said that silence was a sweeter accolade than the many honors heaped on him later in life.

Dad Brown was a down-to-earth man who lived a big life... in a complex world. Yet little meant more to him than his simple choice of believing.

In retrospect, building a bridge seems like an obvious and elementary solution. A simple choice for connecting the two parts of the great State of Michigan. But it took the faith of one cardigan-wearing, pink-mint-eating grandfather to make it so.

There is only one choice.

God is good.
God is real.
God is light.

There is only one choice.

It is that simple. Cross the bridge that carries you toward leading the life where you are not the center, but rather you let love and faithfulness and goodness guide you home to the bay of faith.

There is only one choice.

It is that simple. When you are standing on the shores and looking out onto the bay of life, why would you choose to believe that's all there is, when God is right there waiting to welcome you to put down roots in his peninsula of potential?

There is only one choice.

It is that simple. Live a down-to-earth big life in this complex world. Let your heart and history be rooted in the commonplace. And with humility, believe.

There is only one choice.

It is that simple.

For Further Reflection

Do you use your simple intuition when tackling faith's complex
    questions?
How has God informed your uncomplicated logic?
How has your simple deduction of believing in God been an
    enriching gift?

Put It into Practice

Face your faith questions with a simple heart. Humbly surrender
to the greatness of God and witness how much deeper your
life will become. He wants to give you all things, for His glory
and your joy. Believe it.

Epilogue

Writing this book has been such a surprise to me. It is not something I ever thought I would find myself doing. At the same time, it seems that writing this book has been something I have been preparing for my whole life.

The truth is, if there was anything else that I could have done at this point in my life, I would have jumped at the chance to do that and not this. My Lord took every other single option off my table so that I would sit long enough to find the words to express the gifts I have described throughout this book. God delivered a series of circumstances that forced me to take the time, to feel the need, to tune into the part of me that had to write these words.

I was so often confused and perplexed and lost as I plotted through the best way to tell my stories. So often I felt ashamed by my lack of theological training. So often I felt that I did not have the scholastic ability to articulate well the blessings I wanted to highlight. My intellect felt far too dim to really shine a proper light on the important work of inspiring people to see the divine in the everyday.

And yet we persisted. Day in and day out for the past year, I felt God's blessing as I plotted through the gut-wrenching and glorious reliving that enabled me to retell the moments that allowed me to *Dare to See*.

It is with the utmost humility that I present to you my

moments, my revelations, and my musings with the hope that by unfolding mine, it might lead you to *Dare to See* it in yours.

For after the process of writing this book, I am now surer than ever of my heartfelt, hard-wrought determination that a life of staying tuned into faith by daring to see God's hands in it is a life full of unimaginable blessings.

Acknowledgments

The writing of this book has been such an amazing journey. This journey would have never begun without the example of my mother, Meg Brown's continuous quest to understand deeply the teachings in the Bible. She walks the walk with a devotion to growing closer to the Lord every single day. She would wake up at 5 a.m. most mornings to write her own personal faith-based devotions to read to us over breakfast. This was the beginning of my training of how to discover God in the everyday. While I wrote this book, she tirelessly got on the phone no matter what the hour or what she was doing to hear any and all of my newly completed stories. She cautioned me when I was heavy-handed and pushed me when I had not gone deep enough.

Thank you, Mom. This book would not be without your love and support.

Thanks a million times over…

To my husband, William, who covered for me while I disappeared into myself to write this book. YOU are my everything.

To Prentiss, for propping me up with your enthusiasm and pride when I felt inadequate.

To my sisters, Lynnie and Marlee, and brother, Binger, who are always waiting in the wings, ready to jump whenever needed.

To Nic, Dan, Bob, and all my nieces and nephews. You color the words in this book in so many ways.

To my father, Paul Brown, whose stern hand has softened into the arm around my shoulder that shepherds me forward.

To my beautiful family-in-law. Especially Patt Corbin, who supported the writing of this book with her usual generous quiet strength despite the subject.

To Bridget Johnson, for knowing that you heard something that morning that could grow and be shared. For believing, for brainstorming, and for existing on a similar spiritual page.

To Dylan Seth, you should know I had your note tucked away in my writing book through this entire process. I read it often to remind myself that I had inspired someone. Keep acknowledging your faith-filled moments.

To Kendra Seth and Sarah Easley, who sat on folding chairs and cheered me on that cold March morning.

To my friends, who showed me patience and support as I wrote and worked my way down this path.

To Hachette Publishing and the entire team at FaithWords, for taking a chance on this non-theologian, Sunday-loving, twelve-year-old muffin maker.

To Jody Waldrup, for making magic.

To my editor, Keren Baltzer, who rocked my world with the incredible direction, intelligence, and grace you brought to this project. You made my book so much more better! I am forever grateful.

To the WinSome Women Retreats, for asking me to get up and tell my stories.

To the Congregational Church of Ridgefield, who welcomed and taught my family with such open and hospitable arms. Thank you for creating a place and a space and asking me to showcase my faith. Because, without that, I would not have this.

Finally thank you to all those whose life, love, lessons, and examples fill these pages.

George Ventres, for moving over just enough to let me sit close.

Prentiss Marsh Brown, for always standing tall.

Meredith Robards Hyatt, for seeing me.

Maxine Joyce "Micki" King, for diving deep.

Terri and Michael Lindvall and The Brick Presbyterian Church of New York City, for supporting our marriage and young family.

Norman Rockwell, for turning everyday into art.

Philippe Starck, for teaching me an oh-so-important element when designing a lifestyle.

The AME church of Los Angeles, for hosting the best church party ever.

The United Methodist Church of Petoskey, for nurturing me with so many layers.

Bobby Flay, for continually teaching me the beauty of loyalty especially when life hands you broken plates.

Lou and Sue Chadwick, for showing me the limbs of growth.

Ruth Evashevski, Moey Brown, and my entire collection of aunts, uncles, and cousins, for growing me up.

Arnold Singer, for making me understand there was wisdom in my naïveté.

Frank Cornell, for seating me in just the right place to see.

For almost two decades, KATIE BROWN has transformed the art of homemade into a worldwide brand, delivering how-to information for people passionate about cooking, gardening, crafting, decorating, entertaining, and family. Her enthusiasm, humor, and down-home, all-American personality bring delight to her audiences and instill trust in her brand. *People Magazine* has hailed Katie as "TV's meat-and-potatoes Martha Stewart," and *USA Today* calls her "the doyenne of domesticity for a new generation." In a *Guideposts* cover story, she was described as a "laid-back lifestyle expert." She and her husband live with their two daughters in Santa Monica, California.